HOUSING ISSUES, LAWS AND PROGRAMS

HUD-ASSISTED HOUSING PRESERVATION

HOUSING ISSUES, LAWS AND PROGRAMS

Additional books in this series can be found on Nova's website under the Series tab.

Additional E-books in this series can be found on Nova's website under the E-books tab.

HOUSING ISSUES, LAWS AND PROGRAMS

HUD-ASSISTED HOUSING PRESERVATION

JACQUELINE P. MORAN
AND
ANDREW V. DAVIES
EDITORS

Nova Science Publishers, Inc.
New York

For permission to use material from this book please contact us:
Telephone 631-231-7269; Fax 631-231-8175
Web Site: http://www.novapublishers.com

Library of Congress Cataloging-in-Publication Data

HUD-assisted housing preservation / editors, Jacqueline P. Moran and Andrew V. Davies.
p. cm.
Includes a CRS report for Congress prepared for members and Committees of Congress, and hearings before the House Subcommittee on Housing and Community Opportunity.
Includes index.
ISBN 978-1-61324-856-0 (pbk.)
1. Housing policy--United States. 2. Public housing--Law and legislation--United States. 3. Rental housing--Law and legislation--United States. 4. Housing subsidies--Law and legislation--United States. 5. United States. Dept. of Housing and Urban Development. I. Moran, Jacqueline P. II. Davies, Andrew V. III. United States. Congress. House. Committee on Banking and Financial Services. Subcommittee on Housing and Community Opportunity.
HD7293.H8185 2011
363.5'83--dc23
2011017308

Published by Nova Science Publishers, Inc. † New York

CONTENTS

PREFACE

The term "assisted housing preservation" refers to public policy efforts to maintain the affordability of rental properties financed or subsidized by the Department of Housing and Urban Development (HUD), but owned by private for-profit or nonprofit organizations. Beginning in the late 1950s, HUD extended mortgage and/or rental assistance to owners in exchange for which the owners agreed to make their units affordable to low- and, in some cases, moderate-income tenants. This book introduces the concept of assisted housing preservation, provides background information, and discusses current public policy issues and proposed legislation corresponding to the preservation of HUD-assisted housing.

Chapter 1- The term “assisted housing preservation” refers to public policy efforts to maintain the affordability of rental properties financed or subsidized by the Department of Housing and Urban Development (HUD) but owned by private for-profit or nonprofit organizations. Beginning in the late 1950s, HUD extended mortgage and/or rental assistance to owners, in exchange for which the owners agreed to make their units affordable to low- and, in some cases, moderate-income tenants. The agreements to maintain affordability, sometimes called “affordability restrictions,” were to last between 20 years and 50 years depending on the program. When these affordability restrictions come to an end, owners have the option to stop providing affordable housing to tenants. In some, but not all, cases, tenants living in units that are leaving the assisted housing stock receive housing vouchers that are meant to prevent their displacement.

Chapter 2- This is an edited, reformatted and augmented version of a Testimony given by Tammye Trevino, Administrator, Rural Housing Service,

U.S. Department of Agriculture, Before the Subcommittee on Housing and Community Opportunity, on July 15, 2009.

Chapter 3- This is an edited, reformatted and augmented version of a Statement given by Toby Halliday Vice President, National Housing Trust Presented to the Subcommittee on Housing and Community Opportunity House Committee on Financial Services, on July 15, 2009.

Chapter 4- This is an edited, reformatted and augmented version of a Statement given by Ricky Leung, Treasurer, National Alliance of HUD Tenants, Before the Subcommittee on Housing and Community Opportunity, Hearing on "Affordable Housing Preservation and Protection of Tenants", on July 15, 2009.

Chapter 5- This is an edited, reformatted and augmented version of a Testimony of the Institute for Responsible Housing Preservation Presented by Sarah Metherell Vice President, Steadfast Companies Financial Services Committee Subcommittee on Housing and Community Opportunity U.S. House pf Representatives Hearing on Affordable Housing Preservation, on July 15, 2009.

In: HUD-Assisted Housing Preservation ISBN: 978-1-61324-856-0
Editors: J. Moran and A. Davies

Chapter 1

PRESERVATION OF HUD-ASSISTED HOUSING*

Maggie McCarty and Libby Perl

SUMMARY

The term "assisted housing preservation" refers to public policy efforts to maintain the affordability of rental properties financed or subsidized by the Department of Housing and Urban Development (HUD) but owned by private for-profit or nonprofit organizations. Beginning in the late 1950s, HUD extended mortgage and/or rental assistance to owners, in exchange for which the owners agreed to make their units affordable to low- and, in some cases, moderate-income tenants. The agreements to maintain affordability, sometimes called "affordability restrictions," were to last between 20 years and 50 years depending on the program. When these affordability restrictions come to an end, owners have the option to stop providing affordable housing to tenants. In some, but not all, cases, tenants living in units that are leaving the assisted housing stock receive housing vouchers that are meant to prevent their displacement.

Properties at issue in assisted housing preservation were developed through various programs. HUD provided mortgage assistance or direct loans to owners through the Section 202 loan program and the Section

* This is an edited, reformatted and augmented version of a Congressional Research Service publication 7-5700, R41182, dated January 3, 2011.

236 and Section 221(d)(3) Below Market Interest Rate (BMIR) mortgage insurance programs, all named for the sections of the housing acts under which they were created. HUD also subsidized tenant rents through programs such as the Rent Supplement program, the Rental Assistance Payment program, and the Section 8 project-based rental-assistance program. In some cases, owners received both mortgage financing assistance and rental assistance.

Property owners that received mortgage financing assistance can end their federal obligation to provide affordable housing early by prepaying their mortgages (in some cases), or end it when the mortgage terms come to an end. Owners that entered into rental-assistance contracts with HUD can choose not to renew their contracts when they end. In some cases, HUD can choose to terminate assistance contracts with owners when properties are in poor physical or financial condition. In the past, Congress attempted to reduce the number of property owners that leave HUD-assisted housing programs by restricting owners' abilities to prepay their mortgages. However, these laws (known by their acronyms, ELIHPA and LIHPRHA) faced legal challenges and are no longer in effect. Currently, the primary preservation tool available to HUD is the ability to restructure debt and rental assistance in Section 8 contracts, as authorized by the Multifamily Assisted Housing Reform and Accountability Act (MAHRA).

There have been several proposals to expand the tools available to HUD to help preserve assisted housing. Recent proposals would, in general, focus on incentives to owners to remain in HUD programs or to encourage "preservation purchasers" to buy the properties and maintain affordability. However, any new incentives will require additional funding. In a limited funding environment, questions regarding preservation include whether all properties can and should be preserved, and, if not, which should be the highest priority.

This report introduces the concept of assisted housing preservation, provides background information, and discusses current public policy issues and proposed legislation, including H.R. 4868, the Housing Preservation and Tenant Protection Act, which was reported out of the House Financial Services Committee, but not enacted before the end of the 111th Congress; and S. 118, the Section 202 Supportive Housing for the Elderly Act, which was enacted by the 111th Congress.

INTRODUCTION

The Department of Housing and Urban Development (HUD) has provided housing assistance for low-income households through numerous programs.[1] In some programs, HUD provided assistance by entering into financial arrangements with private owners (both for-profit and nonprofit), who in turn developed and continue to own rental housing projects. In exchange for assistance from HUD, owners agreed to provide affordable housing to tenants for a period of time, anywhere from 20 to 50 years depending on the program. These HUD programs are no longer active, but they created hundreds of thousands of units of affordable housing from the late 1950s through the late 1980s, and these units continue to provide affordable housing to nearly 1.4 million families.

The affordability terms agreed to by property owners participating in these programs, sometimes referred to as "affordability restrictions," began to come to an end in the 1980s. When the restrictions on these properties end, there is a risk that they will become unaffordable to low- and moderate-income tenants, and that those tenants will be displaced. Efforts to maintain the affordability of the remaining HUD-assisted properties as their affordability restrictions come to an end are often referred to as "assisted housing preservation."

This report focuses on assisted housing preservation efforts involving six specific HUD programs, three of which provided financing assistance to private owners through low-interest loans and/or mortgage insurance, and three of which provided rental assistance to owners. These programs were often used in combination with each other, with a property owner receiving both financing assistance and rental assistance.

The following financing assistance programs are covered in this report:

- The *Section 202 loan program,* active from 1959 to 1990. HUD extended low-interest, direct loans to property owners for durations of 40 or 50 years. The Section 202 loan program helped finance the development of approximately 216,000 units of affordable housing; today, about 145,000 units are in properties that still have active loans.
- The *Section 221(d)(3) BMIR (Below Market Interest Rate) program,* active from 1961 to 1968. HUD provided mortgage insurance for low-interest, 40-year loans to private developers. The Section 221(d)(3) BMIR program helped finance the creation of approximately 159,000 units of affordable housing, more than 15,000 of which are in properties that still have active loans insured through the BMIR program.
- The *Section 236 program,* active from 1968 to 1974. HUD provided mortgage insurance for 40-year loans along with mortgage subsidy payments to private developers. The Section 236 program helped

finance the development of approximately 400,000 units of affordable housing, more than 150,000 of which are in properties that still have active loans insured through the Section 236 program.

The following rental-assistance programs are also covered in this report.

- The *Rent Supplement program*, active from 1965 to 1973. HUD provided long-term (up to 40 years) rental-assistance contracts to owners of properties with HUD-assisted financing. Most Rent Supplement contracts were converted to Section 8 project-based contracts (described below), although nearly 13,000 units continue to receive Rent Supplement assistance.
- The *Rental Assistance Payment (RAP) program*, active in the mid-1970s. HUD provided long-term (up to 40 years) rental-assistance contracts to owners of Section 236 properties. Most RAP contracts have been converted to Section 8 assistance (described below), although nearly 16,000 units continue to receive RAP assistance.
- The *Section 8 project-based program,* active from 1974 to 1983. HUD provided long-term (up to 40 years) rental-assistance contracts to owners of newly constructed or substantially rehabilitated properties, as well as existing properties (including Section 202, Section 221(d)(3) BMIR, and Section 236 properties). Roughly 1.2 million units continue to receive Section 8 project-based rental assistance.

While other affordable housing programs also face expiring use restrictions, this report focuses on these six programs for several reasons: (1) Many of the property owners are private for-profit organizations that may have interests other than providing affordable housing when their affordability restrictions come to an end. This contrasts with, for example, the Public Housing program, where owners are quasi-governmental entities whose primary purpose is providing affordable housing. (2) The majority of the affordability restrictions in these six programs will come to an end during the next 5-15 years, depending on the program. This contrasts with newer housing production programs, such as the Section 202 Supportive Housing for the Elderly capital grants program, the Section 811 Supportive Housing for Persons with Disabilities program, or Low Income Housing Tax Credits, where affordability restrictions may extend many years into the future. (3) In past years, Congress has enacted laws that attempted to address housing preservation related to many of these six programs. These attempts met with varying success.

This report does not address the programs of the Department of Agriculture's Rural Housing Service.

Figure 1 illustrates the universe of rental units that were created as part of the six programs discussed in this report. The large circle in the center represents the housing units that receive rental assistance through the Section 8, Rent Supplement, and RAP programs. The circle on the left represents housing units that continue to have active financing through the Section 221(d)(3) BMIR and Section 236 mortgage insurance programs, and the circle on the right represents units that continue to have active financing through the Section 202 loan program. As can be seen in the diagram, the area of overlap between the left and center circles represents Section 221(d)(3) BMIR and Section 236 units that also receive some form of rental assistance, while the overlap between the right and center circles shows Section 202 units that receive some form of rental assistance.[2] See also *Table A-1*, in *Appendix A*, which provides a summary of the properties at issue in assisted housing preservation and their characteristics.

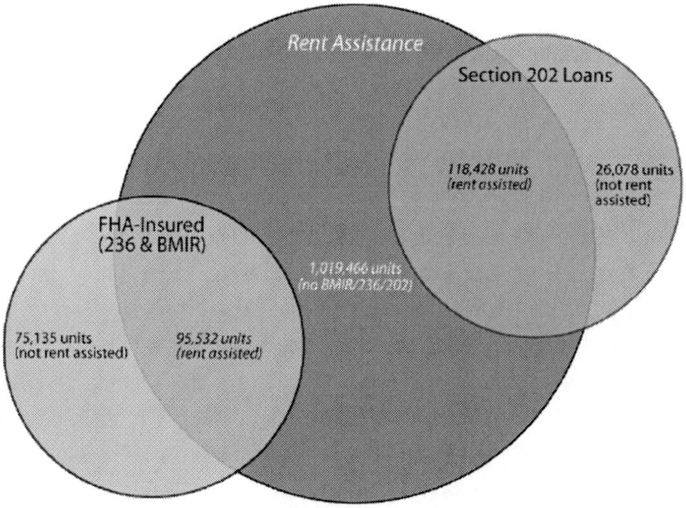

Source: Property and Unit counts are based on CRS analysis of HUD data from the Multifamily Assistance and Section 8 Contracts Database, the Insured Multifamily Mortgages Database, and the 202 Direct Loans database, as of September 30, 2009.

Figure 1. Types of Units at Issue in Assisted Housing Preservation.

This report is divided into six main sections. The first section provides greater detail about the six programs for which housing preservation is an issue. The second section describes how affordability restrictions come to an end. In the case of financing assistance, this can occur through mortgage prepayment or maturation, and in the case of rental assistance, it can occur when contracts expire. And in cases of both financing and rental assistance, properties may become unavailable as affordable housing due to physical deterioration. The second section also discusses what happens to tenants when affordability restrictions end. In the third section, the report describes efforts by both Congress and HUD to extend affordability restrictions in these programs. Some of these efforts have been successful, and some have not. The fourth section discusses preservation priorities—factors that interested parties (owners, tenants, local communities, HUD, Members of Congress) may take into consideration when determining whether a property should be preserved as assisted housing. In the fifth section, the report presents data about the numbers of properties and units of housing involved in the six programs discussed throughout the report. The final section of the report discusses various options regarding how to preserve assisted housing, including current legislation.

Additionally, a review and summary of the properties at issue can be found in *Appendix A*, and a glossary of key terms can be found in *Appendix B*.

PROPERTIES AT ISSUE

Numerous HUD programs have used subsidies to private owners as a way to develop affordable rental housing units. HUD first began to interact with private developers and owners in the early 1960s, largely by providing low-interest loans, and later, Federal Housing Administration (FHA) insurance on mortgages, to developers so that they would have lower debt payments and would in turn be able to charge lower rents to tenants. Units in developments that resulted from these arrangements were considered rent restricted, with property owners agreeing to keep rents at an affordable level. Later, primarily with the creation of Section 8 project-based rental assistance in 1974, the federal government began to pay a portion of tenant rents directly to owners. In some cases, property owners received both financing and rental assistance from HUD. This section of the report discusses six HUD programs through which private owners (both for-profit and nonprofit) received assistance from HUD and for which housing preservation is now a concern.

Financing Assistance (Mortgage Loan and/or Insurance Assistance)

For a number of years during the 1960s and 1970s, HUD subsidized the production of affordable housing through incentives to private developers, including low-interest direct loans and, later, mortgage insurance through the Federal Housing Administration (FHA).[3] The loan and mortgage insurance assistance was meant to lower building owners' costs so that the owners could charge rents that would be affordable to low- and moderate-income families. In exchange for HUD assistance, building owners agreed to maintain their properties' affordability for a period of time—generally anywhere from 20 to 50 years. The primary programs that used these incentives were the Section 202 loan program, the Section 221(d)(3) BMIR program, and the Section 236 program, each named for the section of the housing acts under which they were created. Although most of these units did not initially receive rental assistance, over the years HUD has provided rental assistance for some units to ensure that they are affordable to low-income households. (See discussion under "Rental Assistance" later in this report.)

Section 202 Loan Program

The Section 202 Supportive Housing for the Elderly program,[4] enacted as part of the Housing Act of 1959 (P.L. 86-372), was initially a direct loan program in which the government loaned money to nonprofit organizations to develop affordable housing for elderly households—defined as those with a family member age 62 and older. (For-profit entities were not eligible to participate in the Section 202 loan program.) The Section 202 program operated as a direct loan program until 1990, when the structure of the program changed and HUD began to offer capital grants to developers instead of direct loans.[5] This report focuses on the loan program because the affordability restrictions attached to the properties funded by capital grants will not begin to expire until approximately 2030.

The Section 202 loan program had two different phases. From the program's inception until 1974, HUD extended loans with low interest rates (generally 3%) to developers. These pre-1974 loans funded the development of housing for moderate-income, elderly households. Some units were also set aside to serve tenants with disabilities. In exchange for the assistance provided through government loans, building owners agreed to ensure that their units were affordable for 50 years. In 1974, the Housing and Community Development Act (P.L. 93-383) made changes to the Section 202 loan program. The law changed the interest rate charged on government loans from 3% to the U.S. Treasury's cost of borrowing. P.L. 93-383 also made Section 8 project-based rental assistance available to owners so that units would be affordable for low-income tenants. The initial duration of the Section 8 rental-assistance contracts was 20 years. (For more information about Section 8 rental assistance, see the "Section 8 Project-Based Rental Assistance" section of this report.)

The income eligibility for tenants in Section 202 housing varies based on the phase at which a Section 202 property was developed. Units developed in the earliest years of the program, prior to 1962, have no income restrictions. Those developed from 1962 to 1974 serve tenants with low incomes—at or below 80% of area median income. In general, those developed after 1974 serve tenants with low- or very-low incomes—at or below 50% of area median income.

During the loan phase of the Section 202 program (through the early 1990s), approximately 216,204 units were developed.[6] Currently, the number of Section 202 units with active loans (versus those funded through capital grants) is approximately 144,506.[7]

Section 221(D)(3) Below Market Interest Rate Program

The Section 221(d)(3) Below Market Interest Rate (BMIR) program[8] was enacted as part of the Housing Act of 1961 (P.L. 87-70) in order to provide housing for those families with incomes too high for public housing but too low for market-rate rents.[9] Through the program, private lenders extended FHA-insured loans with interest rates of 3% and durations of up to 40 years to developers of multifamily rental housing projects of at least five units.[10] Lenders then sold the mortgages to the Federal National Mortgage Association (Fannie Mae).[11] The program continued until 1968, when the Section 236 program replaced it as a vehicle for producing multifamily housing for low-income families.

Section 221(d)(3) BMIR units are available to households with incomes up to 95% of the area median income.[12] HUD approves a BMIR rent for each property, and that rent is set and adjusted based on the budget for the property, including actual operating costs, debt service, and any allowable dividend. Most residents pay the BMIR rent; however, if, after moving in, a tenant's income increases and exceeds 110% of the BMIR income limit, then the household must pay 110% of the BMIR rent.[13] Some units are subsidized to assist tenants with low incomes through the Rent Supplement Program, though many Rent Supplement subsidies have been converted to Section 8 project-based assistance.[14]

The Section 221(d)(3) BMIR program created approximately 159,000 units in 845 properties.[15] Today, there are roughly 15,218 units in 124 properties with active Section 221(d)(3) BMIR financing.[16]

Section 236 Program

The Section 236 program[17] was enacted as part of the Housing and Urban Development Act of 1968 (P.L. 90-448). The program, which was active in providing funds to produce new housing units from 1969 through 1973,[18] provided mortgage insurance to housing developers for the construction and rehabilitation of multifamily housing that would be affordable to low- and moderate-income families.[19] Private nonprofit organizations, limited dividend corporations, and cooperative housing corporations were eligible to participate. In addition to mortgage insurance, the program provided (and continues to provide) mortgage subsidies to building owners through a mechanism called Interest Reduction Payments (IRPs).[20] At the time developers built their housing, they borrowed funds at the market interest rate. The government then provided an IRP subsidy that ensured that owners would only pay a 1% interest rate on their mortgages.[21] The low interest payments were meant to reduce the financing costs paid by owners, which would, in turn, permit owners to pass the savings on to tenants by charging lower, more affordable rents.[22] Contracts between HUD and building owners for IRPs were initially supposed to last 40 years.[23] However, in order to attract developers to the Section 236 program, some contracts enabled owners to prepay their mortgages after 20 years.[24]

The Section 236 program serves households with low incomes—those earning 80% or less of the area median income—although owners may admit over-income tenants in certain circumstances.[25] Tenants pay one of two rent levels: basic rent or market rate rent, depending on income. The basic rent is the amount the owners need to support the facilities at a 1% mortgage interest rate.[26] Market rate rent is the amount needed to support the facilities at the mortgage interest rate without the IRPs. Both the basic rent and market rent are set by the property owner based on the budget of the individual property and are subject to HUD's approval.[27] Tenants pay the basic rent or 30% of their income, whichever is higher, but rent cannot exceed the market rate. In addition, some tenants in Section 236 housing have their rents subsidized. HUD initially provided subsidies through either the Rent Supplement or Rental Assistance Payment (RAP) programs, but when Section 8 project-based assistance was introduced in 1974, many of the subsidies were converted to Section 8 assistance.[28] (See the "Rent-Assisted Units" section of this report for more information.)

The Section 236 program created approximately 400,000 units of affordable housing in more than 3,600 properties;[29] today, approximately 155,449 units in 1,418 properties continue to be insured through the Section 236 program.[30] As many as 249,000 units continue to receive IRPs;[31] this number is higher than the number of insured units as a result of IRP "decoupling," a process in which owners may prepay their insured mortgages and continue to receive IRPs. The process is discussed later in this report, in the section "IRP Decoupling."

RENTAL ASSISTANCE

As discussed previously, the early federal housing programs provided financing assistance to private developers of affordable housing with the idea that the reduced capital and/or debt service costs would allow owners to charge low rents that would be affordable to lower-income families. Over time, it became clear that the financing assistance was not sufficient to make rents low enough to be affordable to the poorest families while still maintaining the financial viability of the properties. In order to more deeply target housing assistance to the poorest families while also ensuring that property owners received sufficient rental income to successfully operate their properties, the federal government began providing rental assistance contracts to private property owners for all or a portion of their units. The rental assistance contracts—referred to as project-based rental assistance because the assistance is tied to specific units in a project—permitted tenants to pay a lower, income-based rent, with the federal government making up the difference between a tenant's contribution and the rent for the unit, as set by HUD. With the creation of the Section 8 project-based rental assistance program in the mid-1970s, rental-assistance contracts became the primary form of federal assistance for new affordable multifamily housing developments until the program was ended in the mid-1980s.

The Rent Supplement Program

The Rent Supplement program[32] was enacted as part of the Housing and Urban Development Act of 1965 (P.L. 89-117) to subsidize the rent payments of low-income households living in certain federally assisted properties, including those with Section 221(d)(3) mortgage insurance and Section 202 loans.[33] Under the Rent Supplement program, HUD entered into contracts with building owners to make up the difference between 25% of tenant income (later raised to 30%) and the rent for the unit.[34] Generally, up to 20% of units in a building were eligible for Rent Supplement payments, although the Housing and Urban Development Act of 1969 (P.L. 91-152) made up to 40% of units eligible for subsidy payments if the HUD Secretary determined it was necessary.[35] Rent Supplement contracts were written for the duration of the HUD-insured mortgage.[36]

The Rent Supplement program was suspended in 1973 when President Nixon imposed a moratorium on the new construction of subsidized housing (the "Nixon Moratorium"). Most Rent Supplement contracts were converted to Section 8 contracts in the mid-1980s.[37] The main exception was properties that were financed with state funds rather than an FHA-insured mortgage. At its peak, the Rent Supplement program assisted 179,908 units.[38] Between conversions to Section 8 and contract expirations, there are far fewer contracts today. According to HUD, the remaining Rent Supplement contracts are primarily found in state-aided properties.[39] Today, there are about 12,847 Rent Supplement units.[40]

The Rental Assistance Payment (RAP) Program

In the Housing and Community Development Act of 1974 (P.L. 93-383), Congress created the Rental Assistance Payment (RAP) program.[41] The RAP program was designed to provide additional rental-assistance contracts to Section 236 properties. As with Rent Supplement contracts, RAP contracts were meant to allow property owners to serve lower-income families than they otherwise might be able to serve. Since no new Section 236 commitments were entered into following the Nixon Moratorium, RAP contracts were made available to existing Section 236 properties. RAP contracts were limited to 20% of a property's units (or more at the discretion of the Secretary),[42] and were written for the duration of the FHA-insured mortgage or 40 years, whichever was shorter.[43]

As with the Rent Supplement program, most RAP contracts were converted to Section 8 contracts in the mid-1980s. Today, there are about 15,870 RAP units remaining.[44]

Section 8 Project-Based Rental Assistance

In addition to creating the Rental Assistance Payment program for existing Section 236 properties, the Housing and Community Development Act of 1974 also created a new program called the Section 8 program.[45] The Section 8 program consisted of three components: new construction, substantial rehabilitation, and existing housing certificates. The first two components were designed to promote the development of new housing, whereas the latter was designed to subsidize rents in the existing housing stock. Later, HUD expanded the use of Section 8 project-based rental assistance by making it available to properties with HUD financing assistance, including those with Section 202 loans and Section 221(d)(3) and Section 236 mortgage insurance.

New Construction, Substantial Rehabilitation, Existing Housing

Under the new construction and substantial rehabilitation components of the early Section 8 program, HUD entered into long-term (20- or 40-year) contracts[46] with private property owners who were willing to construct new units or rehabilitate older ones to house low- and very low-income tenants. Owners could be for-profit or nonprofit entities and the contracts could cover all or part of the units in their developments. Some of these new properties were financed with FHA-insured mortgages, some were financed with state-based financing, and some were built without insured or assisted financing.

Under the Section 8 program, HUD agreed to make housing assistance payments (HAP) toward each unit covered under the contract for the duration of the contract. Those assistance payments made up the difference between a previously agreed-upon rent and the tenants' required contribution toward rent (initially 25%—later raised to 30%—of their adjusted income). The rents were generally not to exceed 110% of the Fair Market Rent (FMR) established by HUD, although they could go as high as 20% above FMR if the Secretary determined it to be necessary in special circumstances.[47] In order to receive assistance, all assisted units had to be rented to low-income families, and some proportion of the units had to be rented to very low-income families.[48]

The existing housing portion of the Section 8 program—also called the Section 8 certificate program—was tenant-based, meaning that the assistance was tied to a tenant rather than a unit. Under the certificate program, HUD would provide the local public housing authorities (PHAs) that own and manage public housing with renewable contracts[49] for a specified number of certificates. PHAs would then award those certificates to eligible families, who could use them to rent the housing of their choice in the private market. HUD would pay the difference between the tenant's contribution toward the rent (30% of family income) and the rent for the unit. The contract rent was generally limited to the HUD-set FMR for the area.[50]

The Housing and Community Development Amendments of 1978 (P.L. 95-557) added a moderate rehabilitation component to the Section 8 program. Under Section 8 Moderate Rehabilitation (Mod-Rehab), rental assistance was provided to projects that were in need of repairs costing at least $1,000 per unit to make the housing decent, safe, and sanitary.[51]

By the early 1980s, concern about the Section 8 program was growing, particularly about the development of new units under the new construction and substantial rehabilitation portions of the program. The program was perceived as having per-unit costs that were too high and development times that were too slow, which was leading to the accumulation of large amounts of unused funding. Concern was also growing about the implications of project-based assistance models, which resulted in properties with high concentrations of poverty. Also, because contracts were written for such long terms, appropriators had to provide large amounts of budget authority each time they funded a new contract. As the budget deficit grew, many Members of Congress became concerned with the high costs associated with Section 8 new construction and substantial rehabilitation, and these segments of the Section 8 program were repealed in the Housing and Urban-Rural Recovery Act of 1983 (P.L. 98-181).[52] The 1983 act also created a new, tenant-based housing voucher program, similar to the Section 8 existing certificate program.[53] The Section 8 existing program was eventually replaced by the Section 8 Housing Choice Voucher program, which is the largest direct housing assistance program in use today.[54]

Additional Uses of Section 8 Project-Based Rental Assistance

Several other forms of Section 8 project-based rental assistance, or uses for existing Section 8 project-based rental assistance, were developed following the 1974 act, several of which were targeted to properties that had been constructed with HUD-assisted financing through the Section 202, Section 221(d)(3)BMIR, and Section 236 programs.

HUD created the *Section 8 Loan Management Set Aside (LMSA)* initiative[55] in 1976 as a way to reduce claims on HUD's FHA insurance fund and to reduce the rent burdens on low-income families.[56] Financially troubled FHA-insured properties (including properties with Section 202 loans and Section 221(d)(3) and Section 236 insured financing) were eligible to apply to receive pay income-based rents (up to 100% of FMR, or 120% with prior HUD permission).[57] The federal government paid the difference between the tenant rents and a rent level necessary to help the property avoid a default and subsequent claim on the FHA fund. Rents could be adjusted annually, or more frequently at HUD's option. Adjustments were based on a written request of an owner or on an Annual Adjustment Factor (AAF).[58] Owners would also be paid 80% of their rent for units vacant for up to 60 days. Section 8 contract terms under LMSA were initially five years, renewable in five-year increments. Congress stopped providing funding for LMSA in FY1994.[59]

The Housing and Community Development Act of 1987 (P.L. 100-242), as a part of broader preservation proposals, required HUD to provide Section 8 contracts in several additional circumstances. Title I[60] required HUD to facilitate the sale to a third party of FHA-insured properties that HUD had acquired through foreclosure.[61] These properties included those financed through the Section 221(d)(3) BMIR program and the Section 236 program. HUD met the requirement by providing rental-assistance contracts to purchasers through the *Section 8 Property Disposition* program. In 1995, HUD stopped entering into new Section 8 property disposition contracts and began using Section 8 tenant-based vouchers once properties were sold.[62]

Title II of the Housing and Community Development Act authorized the provision of new Section 8 contracts as a part of preservation transactions. Under the *Housing Preservation Program*, HUD entered into project-based Section 8 contracts with owners of HUD-assisted multifamily properties (including Section 221(d)(3) and Section 236 insured mortgages) at risk of leaving the affordable housing stock as an incentive to owners keep their properties affordable. The program ran from 1987 to 1996; in 1997, Congress discontinued the use of these contracts as a cost-saving measure and the program was terminated in 1998.[63]

Current Status

While HUD does not have authority to enter into new Section 8 project-based rental-assistance contracts, there are roughly 1.2 million Section 8 project-based units still under contract.[64] Of those units, about two-thirds were subsidized through the new construction, substantial rehabilitation, and moderate rehabilitation versions of Section 8. About a quarter were subsidized through the LMSA version, and about half the remaining units were subsidized through the property disposition and preservation versions.

The Annual Contributions Contracts between owners and HUD describe how many units in an owner's property are subsidized, as well as how the rent level was set and how rent is to be adjusted.[65] Owners are required to maintain their properties according to HUD-set quality standards, and are required, generally, to contribute to a replacement reserve account. For the most part, HUD has contracted with third parties, referred to as Performance-Based Contract Administrators (PBCAs), to manage Section 8 project-based contracts.[66]

As discussed later in this report ("Mark-to-Market and Section 8 Renewal"), when project-based Section 8 contracts expire, the owner can choose to either renew the contract with HUD[67] or leave the program and charge market rents for units. When an owner ends a HAP contract with HUD, the tenants in the building are provided with vouchers designed to allow them to stay in their unit. (See "Implications for Tenants" later in this report.)

How Affordability Restrictions Come to an End

A variety of circumstances may lead owners to stop providing affordable housing and leave HUD subsidized housing programs. In high-rent areas, owners may decide to pay off their assisted mortgages or choose not to renew a Section 8 rental-assistance contract in order to convert a property to market-rate housing or to sell the building at a profit. In cases where a property has been allowed to deteriorate significantly or the owner has violated the HUD program rules in other ways, HUD may choose to end a contract with an owner. This section details these possibilities.

Residual Receipts

In some cases, income from a Section 202, Section 221(d)(3), Section 236, or Section 8 rent-assisted property (rents plus subsidy) is greater than the amount needed to meet the operating costs, debt service, and replacement reserves for the property. Some for-profit owners are permitted to keep all excess income generated from their property. Other for-profit owners, called "limited-dividend" owners, are capped at the amount of excess income they can retain. Nonprofit owners are not permitted to keep excess funding.

In the case of "limited-dividend" for-profit owners, as well as nonprofit owners, excess income must be deposited in a "residual receipts" account. HUD may permit owners to take allocations from the residual receipts account in a limited number of circumstances, such as to make repairs to a property.

At the end of the affordability agreement, except in the case of certain Section 8 properties, any remaining funds in the residual receipts account reverts to the property owner. In the case of certain properties with Section 8 contracts entered into after 1979 (referred to as New Regulation, or New Reg, properties), any remaining funds revert to HUD. (For more information about Residual Receipts, see Chapter 25 of HUD Handbook 4350.1.)

Financing Assistance: Mortgage Prepayment and Maturation

The federal affordability restrictions on assisted housing come to an end when owners prepay their mortgages (if prepayment is an option), when the mortgages mature, or if HUD chooses to terminate its contract with a housing provider. The circumstances under which affordability restrictions may come to an end depend on the program under which the property was developed.

Section 236 and Section 221(d)(3) BMIR

Section 236 and Section 221(d)(3) program contracts can come to an end through both mortgage prepayment and mortgage maturation. In both programs, the initial term of the affordability restrictions was to be 40 years, the same as the duration of the mortgages. However, in order to attract property owners to the programs, HUD inserted clauses in many mortgage contracts allowing owners to prepay their mortgages after 20 years without

HUD approval.[68] The ability to prepay is limited to for-profit owners; units owned by for-profit owners made up about 62% of the total Section 236 housing stock and 59% of the total Section 221(d)(3) BMIR inventory.[69] Because Section 221(d)(3) and Section 236 properties were funded prior to 1974, owners became eligible to prepay by the mid-1990s.

An owner's ability to prepay is also dependent on whether there is a rental-assistance contract attached to all or a portion of the units. Owners with no rental-assistance contracts can prepay the mortgage, at which point tenants receive enhanced Section 8 vouchers that allow them to either stay in their units or move elsewhere. [70] (For more information about enhanced vouchers, see the "Implications for Tenants" section of this report.) Owners with Rent Supplement contracts cannot prepay their mortgages.[71] For owners with Section 8 contracts, rental-assistance payments are to continue through the contract term, at which point the owner can opt out of the Section 8 program. At that point, income-eligible tenants receive enhanced Section 8 vouchers.[72] According to HUD, between 1998 and 2004 approximately 1,409 Section 236 and Section 221(d)(3) BMIR property owners prepaid their mortgages.[73]

Section 236 and Section 221(d)(3) owners also can choose to convert units to market-rate housing at the end of the 40-year mortgage term. At that point, if any Rent Supplement contract is still in place, it will be terminated.[74] Section 8 contracts continue until their expiration, at which point tenants receive enhanced vouchers. If units are not rent assisted, then tenants do not receive Section 8 vouchers upon mortgage maturation.

Section 202 Loan Program

Although Section 202 owners may prepay their loans under certain circumstances, in general, prepayment does not result in the end of affordability restrictions. As part of an FY1984 supplemental appropriations act (P.L. 98-181), Section 202 owners were given the option of prepaying their loans with HUD permission. However, under the law's provisions, owners are required to continue to operate the property through the date of the original loan under terms at least as advantageous to tenants as those under the original loan. The American Homeownership and Economic Opportunity Act of 2000 (P.L. 106-569) added that, if there is a rental-assistance contract in place, the property owner must continue to operate under the terms required by the rental-assistance contract through loan maturity.[75] Then, in 2010 the Section 202 Supportive Housing for the Elderly Act (S. 118) provided that HUD would approve prepayment of existing Section 202 loans if owners agreed to maintain affordability under the terms of the original loan or existing project-based rental assistance contract for 20 years *beyond* the date of the original loan's maturation.

While most Section 202 owners may only prepay their loans with HUD permission, there is an exception for some properties that were financed between 1977 and 1982 where owners had written into the contract the right to prepay their loans without permission from HUD.[76] However, because most Section 202 units financed during this time period also received Section 8 assistance, prepayment does not necessarily mean an end to tenant assistance because Section 8 rental-assistance contracts continue in place until contract expiration.[77] If units have Rent Supplement contracts, those contracts terminate at the time of prepayment and tenants receive regular Section 8 vouchers.[78] If owners with the right to prepay without notice choose instead to follow HUD guidelines and give notice of intent to prepay, then the Rent Supplement and Section 8 contracts continue in place.[79]

40- or 50-year maturation period. As with the Section 236 and Section 221(d)(3) programs, if any Rent Supplement contract is in place, it will be terminated at the end of the loan. Section 8 contracts continue until their expiration, at which point tenants receive enhanced vouchers if owners choose not to renew. If units are not rent assisted, then tenants do not receive Section 8 vouchers upon mortgage maturation.

Rental Assistance: Expiring Rental-Assistance Contracts

Section 8

When Section 8 project-based housing assistance payment (HAP) contracts expire, the property owner can, generally, either renew the contract with HUD or leave the program. If the owner chooses not to renew the contract, and faces no further restrictions on the property,[80] the owner can choose to charge whatever rent the market will bear,[81] or sell or convert the property to another use. As discussed later in this report, a number of factors can influence a property owner's decision to either stay in the Section 8 program or to leave, such as the state of the housing market, other available options, and the mission/profit orientation of the owner. However, if the property is in poor condition, then the owner may not have the option to renew the contract, as HUD may choose not to renew.

When a HAP contract with HUD ends, the tenants in the building are provided with some form of voucher designed to either allow them to stay in their unit or move to a new home.

According to a HUD analysis, from 1998-2004, owners of over 11,000 properties (nearly 800,000 units) chose to renew their Section 8 contracts and owners of 1,363 properties (nearly 80,000 units) chose to opt-out of their Section 8 contract. Another 1,367 properties (almost 110,000 units) had been foreclosed upon or enforcement action had been taken.[82]

RAP and Rent Supplement

Unlike Section 8 project-based rental assistance, HUD has no authority to renew RAP and Rent Supplement contracts when they expire. These contracts generally expire at the same time that the assisted mortgages mature. Upon expiration, tenants being assisted under RAP contracts are not eligible for tenant protection vouchers; tenants being assisted under Rent Supplement contracts are eligible for tenant protection vouchers, and in some cases, enhanced vouchers.[83]

Troubled Properties

Another way that properties can leave the assisted housing stock is when HUD chooses to sever the contract with a troubled property or through an owner's default on an FHA-insured mortgage or HUD loan. HUD regularly assesses both the physical and financial health of the multifamily insured and assisted housing stock through its Real Estate Assessment Center (REAC).

As a condition of receiving mortgage assistance, rental assistance, or both, property owners agree to maintain their properties according to both local building codes and HUD's Uniform Physical Condition Standards (UPCS).[84] If owners fail to maintain their properties, HUD can find them in default of their contracts.

Properties are periodically inspected to ensure that they comply with the UPCS.[85] Based on the findings of those inspections, each property is assigned a numeric score.[86] Any score below 60 is considered at risk,[87] and these properties are referred to the Departmental Enforcement Center (DEC).[88] Once a property has been referred to the DEC, the owner meets with the DEC staff and then has 60 days to make repairs necessary to raise the score above the failing point. If the owner cannot or will not repair the property within 60 days, then HUD will find the property in default of its assistance contract. When a property defaults on its contract, HUD has a number of options. In the case of a project-based rental-assistance property, HUD can choose to abate, or end, the Section 8 contract and issue vouchers to the tenants. In the case of a property with an assisted mortgage, HUD can choose to pursue foreclosure of the property and take ownership. HUD can also encourage the owner to pursue a transfer of the property to another owner. Federal regulations give HUD broad flexibility to use its discretion in these cases.[89]

According to HUD's FY2009 Performance and Accountability Report, 93.3% of privately owned, HUD-insured properties met HUD's physical condition standards in FY2009.[90] While the majority of the stock passed inspection, some units among those that failed were found to have multiple exigent health and safety concerns.[91]

HUD can also choose to take action against a property owner for financial reasons. All owners of HUD-insured, HUD-held, and assisted properties must submit annual financial statement and audit information to REAC.[92] REAC reviews the statements to determine the financial health of properties in their various portfolios, protect the Department from financial loss (through claims on the FHA insurance fund), ensure proper use of revenues and federal subsidies, and assess owner compliance with Business Agreements (e.g., use restrictions, Housing Assistance Payment Contracts, etc.).[93]

If an owner is found to be improperly managing its federal funds in the program, then HUD can find the owner in default of the assistance contract and take action against the owner. That action could include financial penalties, but could also lead HUD to terminate the assistance contract. Again, HUD has broad discretion in determining how to handle properties with financial irregularities. According to HUD's FY2009 Performance and Accountability Report, 98.6% of multifamily assisted and/or insured properties had no compliance issues or audit findings, or had any such issues or findings resolved by the end of the fiscal year.[94]

From 1998 through 2004, according to HUD, 2,385 properties with 182,945 units had left the assisted housing stock as a result of HUD enforcement action or foreclosure.[95]

IMPLICATIONS FOR TENANTS

In some cases, when an affordability restriction on a HUD-assisted property ends, low-income tenants may receive a rent subsidy to help protect them from rent increases or allow them to move to a new unit and pay an affordable rent.[96] These rent subsidies are provided in the form of Section 8 Housing Choice Vouchers. Families receiving Section 8 vouchers generally pay 30% of their income toward their rent for the unit of their choice in the private market, and HUD makes up the difference between the tenant's payment and rent for the unit. Vouchers are portable, which means if a family chooses to move, they can take their voucher subsidy with them.

When vouchers are provided to families who are losing other forms of HUD-assisted housing (such as when affordability restrictions end), they are referred to as tenant protection vouchers.[97] One difference between tenant protection vouchers and regular Section 8 vouchers is that families who receive tenant protection vouchers must pay at least as much rent as they were paying under their previous assistance program, even if it exceeds 30% of their income. Some tenant protection vouchers, called enhanced vouchers, have special features that allow them to increase to values higher than normally allowed in the voucher program in order to allow families to remain in their units as rents increase.

Tenant protection vouchers are generally provided to families who are losing their assistance as a result of HUD enforcement and property disposition actions (through foreclosure or abatement of a Section 8 contract) and when certain Rent Supplement contracts end (where there is not also a Section 8 project-based contract in place).

Enhanced vouchers are generally provided to families who are losing their assistance because an owner decided to opt-out of renewing a project-based Section 8 rental-assistance contract. Enhanced vouchers are also provided to tenants in certain properties when owners prepay their assisted mortgages. Generally, tenants in properties with mortgages that can be prepaid without prior HUD approval are eligible to receive enhanced voucher assistance. When enhanced vouchers are issued following a prepayment, all eligible families receive a voucher, not just those who were receiving assistance prior to the prepayment. In order to be eligible, families must be low income, or have moderate incomes if they are elderly or disabled, or must live in a low-vacancy area. Enhanced vouchers lose their enhanced nature and convert to regular vouchers when and if a family moves from its original property.

In some cases, families do not receive tenant protection or enhanced vouchers when affordability agreements end. Families who live in properties where the affordability agreement would be terminated upon mortgage prepayment, and prior HUD approval to prepay is required, would not generally receive tenant protection or enhanced vouchers upon mortgage prepayment. The types of properties that fit this category include those with nonprofit owners, those with certain limited-dividend owners,[98] and those with certain for-profit owners, including those with Rent Supplement contracts and those with other assistance.[99] Additionally, families living in properties with maturing mortgages without Section 8 assistance and tenants with assistance through the old Rental Assistance Payment (RAP) program do not currently receive either tenant protection or enhanced vouchers.

PREVIOUS AND ONGOING EFFORTS TO PRESERVE ASSISTED HOUSING

By the mid-1980s, Congress and HUD had become concerned about the potential loss of hundreds of thousands of units of privately owned, assisted housing serving low-income families. Under the direction of Congress and HUD, a "National Housing Preservation Task Force" was convened. The Task Force's final report, issued in 1987, identified four primary threats to the inventory: expiration of rental-assistance contracts, maturation of secondary financing, an aging housing supply with limited incentives for owners to maintain properties, and owners becoming eligible to prepay. Of the more than 2 million units in the assisted housing inventory at the time, the Task Force identified 645,000 as being the most vulnerable to loss.[100]

In response to these concerns about the loss of the assisted housing inventory, Congress enacted several laws that gave private owners of HUD-assisted housing incentives to maintain the affordability of their properties. One of these laws, the Multifamily Assisted Housing Reform and contracts between HUD and property owners. Two other laws, neither of which are currently in effect, addressed mortgage prepayments by private owners. These are the Emergency Low-Income Housing Preservation Act (P.L. 100-242) and the Low-Income Housing Preservation and Resident Homeownership Act (P.L. 101-625). While these laws are no longer in effect, the properties that went through their preservation processes are still governed by the agreements that were established at the time. This section describes these laws and their current status.

FINANCING ASSISTANCE

Emergency Low-Income Housing Preservation Act (ELIHPA)[101]

Congress initially attempted to address mortgage prepayments and the loss of affordable housing units by enacting Title II of the Housing and Community Development Act of 1987 (P.L. 100- 242), the Emergency Low-Income Housing Preservation Act (ELIHPA). The law prevented owners from prepaying their mortgages in many circumstances, and was described by some as a moratorium on mortgage prepayment. ELIHPA was designed to be a temporary measure, and intended to give Congress time to develop a permanent plan for addressing prepayments.

The ELIHPA restrictions applied to owners of properties insured under the Section 236 program, to owners of Section 221(d)(3) market rate properties that also received rental assistance through Section 8 or the Rent Supplement program, owners of Section 221(d)(3) BMIR projects, and those properties held by the HUD Secretary and formerly insured under one of these programs.[102] The law required owners to obtain HUD approval prior to prepayment, even in cases where the mortgage contract allowed prepayment without HUD approval. Owners that wished to prepay their mortgages were required to submit to HUD a notice of intent to prepay, together with a plan explaining their proposed changes to the mortgage, the low-income affordability restrictions, and ownership of the building. The plan was also to include an assessment of how prepayment and other actions would affect existing tenants and how they would affect the general availability of affordable housing in the community.

HUD was to allow the prepayment of the mortgage, along with the termination of affordability restrictions, only if certain conditions were met.

- In cases where comparable affordable housing was not available for current tenants, the plan could not, without good cause, "materially increase economic hardship" or displace current tenants who wanted to stay.

- The prepayment could not affect the supply of decent, safe, and sanitary housing that was affordable for low- and very low-income families in the area, the ability of families to find housing near employment, or the housing opportunities for minorities in the community. Alternatively (if a plan did not meet this requirement), a state and local jurisdiction could approve the plan as being in accordance with the state plan developed pursuant to ELIHPA.

For owners who wanted to maintain affordability or could not meet prepayment requirements, ELIHPA gave HUD the authority to offer incentives to owners to maintain affordability. Among the incentives were an increase in the return that owners could receive on their investment; increased access to residual receipts accounts or project reserves; additional Section 8 assistance[103] or increases in Section 8 rents for units with existing contracts; and capital improvement loans. Owners that accepted incentives agreed to continue providing affordable housing for the period of time covered by the original mortgage—generally an additional 20 years.[104]

ELIHPA's provisions were originally slated to sunset two years after enactment (on February 5, 1990),[105] however, the law was extended by Congress through November 1990, when it was superseded by the Low-Income Housing Preservation and Resident Homeownership Act (described below).[106] However, owners that entered into preservation agreements with HUD under the terms of ELIHPA were bound by the terms of those agreements.[107]

Low-Income Housing Preservation and Resident Homeownership Act (LIHPRHA)

In 1990, Title VI of the Cranston-Gonzalez National Affordable Housing Act (P.L. 101-625), the Low-Income Housing Preservation and Resident Homeownership Act (LIHPRHA), replaced the temporary ELIHPA law with what was intended to be a permanent preservation program.[108] The new program covered the same types of housing developments and, like ELIHPA, limited the occasions on which owners could prepay their mortgages and terminate affordability restrictions, and it also provided incentives for building owners to offer affordable housing. However, LIHPRHA differed from ELIHPA by providing owners with a third potential option: selling their properties to qualified purchasers under certain circumstances.

Regardless of the option an owner selected, LIHPRHA—similar to ELIHPA—instituted requirements that owners notify HUD, state or local governments, and residents of their intent.

Both laws also developed tenant protections for residents whose properties were prepaid or (in the case of LIHPRHA) sold, in the form of Section 8 vouchers.

Option 1: Prepayment

LIHPRHA was similar to ELIHPA in limiting the ability of owners to prepay their mortgages and terminate affordability restrictions. As with ELIHPA, HUD could only permit owners to prepay if HUD determined that the prepayment would not materially increase economic hardship or displace current tenants without good cause, and would not affect the supply of housing for low-income and very low-income households, housing near employment, and housing for minorities.[109] Owners wishing to prepay were required, as they were in ELIHPA, to file a notice of intent to prepay with HUD and to certify that the aforementioned conditions were met. If owners prepaid their mortgages, tenants could remain in the housing at the same rental rates for three years, and if tenants moved, the owners were responsible for paying half of the moving costs.[110]

If owners did not meet these conditions for prepayment, one of three scenarios could occur. An owner could (1) maintain affordability, assisted by incentives from HUD, generally in the form of higher rents; (2) sell the property to a qualified purchaser who would maintain affordability; or (3) prepay the mortgage and convert units to market rate housing, though this was only allowed in a limited number of circumstances—such as when HUD approved a plan for preservation incentives but did not provide them or when no qualified purchaser could be found.

Option 2: Stay in

For owners that chose to stay in the program and maintain their properties as affordable housing—either because they were not permitted to prepay, or because they wanted to remain in the program—LIHPRHA modified the preservation incentives under ELIHPA. The ELIHPA preservation incentives included Section 8 rental assistance, rent increases paid by tenants, HUD-insured loans for equity take-outs, and grants and deferred-payment loans for capital improvements. Under LIHPRHA, some preservation incentives were expanded: the value of Section 8 rents increased to 120% of FMR (from 100% under ELIHPA), and families eligible to receive Section 8 assistance expanded to those at 80% of area median income (up from those at 50% under ELIHPA).[111] However, LIHPRHA limited the amount of assistance that could be provided to a property in other ways. The amount of annual returns an owner could realize was limited to 8% of equity (from no specified limit under ELIHPA), access to residual receipts was limited (there were no restrictions under ELIHPA), and loan limits for owners who stayed in the program were reduced.[112]

Option 3: Sale

LIHPRHA created a third option for property owners: sale to a qualified purchaser—a buyer that would maintain the affordability of the property. This option could occur in situations where owners were not permitted to prepay, where they were unable to receive sufficient preservation incentive funding to stay in, or where they wanted to sell their properties. Owners wishing to pursue this option were also required to submit a notice of intent to HUD.

There were a number of ways in which a sale could occur. (1) In the first six months, owners were required to attempt to find a "priority purchaser" that was either a resident council or community-based nonprofit organization that had the support of the majority of tenants.[113] (2) If no buyer could be found during the first six-month period, during the subsequent six months the owner could sell to any priority purchaser, including nonprofits or state and local housing agencies. (3) If a priority purchaser could not be found, owners could sell to "qualified purchasers"—for-profit entities that agreed to continue providing affordable housing. (4) If an owner could not find a qualified purchaser after three additional months had elapsed, the owner could decide to stay in as the owner of the property and accept incentives, or the owner could sell the building and convert units to market rate rent.[114]

In all sales, LIHPRHA authorized HUD to provide purchasers with rental incentives similar to those received by owners that retained the property.

The End of ELIHPA and LIHPRHA

By the mid-1990s, concern was growing among housing advocates, HUD, and Congress about the cost of HUD's preservation efforts.[115] Under ELIHPA and LIHPRHA, 751 properties with more than 90,000 units had completed plans of action (POAs) and received preservation funding through FY1996.[116] According to GAO testimony in 1995, the average cost to preserve a unit of housing was about $19,000,[117] and a GAO survey of 40 properties found that HUD preservation funding exceeded the value of the properties in more than half of the cases.[118]

In addition to concerns about cost, LIHPRHA presented legal issues. Some property owners contested the provisions of both ELIHPA and LIHPRHA, arguing both that the laws violated the contracts under which the owners had agreed to participate in the program, and that the laws constituted a taking of private property by the government. The lawsuits contesting ELIHPA and LIHPRHA have had varying outcomes. Some have been settled; according to HUD, three cases have been settled and payments of $35 million, $2 million, and $1.25 million have or will be made.[119] Some cases have been decided in favor of owners and some cases continue to be litigated.[120]

In the FY1996 HUD appropriations law, Congress reinstated the right of owners to prepay their mortgages without prior HUD permission, effectively overriding the central provision of LIHPRHA.[121] In the FY1997 appropriations laws, Congress imposed caps on the amount of funding HUD could provide in preservation incentives for owners undergoing LIHPRHA preservation transactions. In FY1998, Congress stopped providing funding to HUD for preservation incentives to owners under LIHPRHA, effectively ending the LIHPRHA program.[122]

IRP Decoupling

When Section 236 owners initially began prepaying their mortgages, the prepayment also brought an end to the interest reduction payments (IRPs). HUD paid IRPs to owners of Section 236 properties to ensure that the effective interest rate on the mortgage was 1%. However, as part of the FY2000 HUD Appropriations Act (P.L. 106-74), Congress implemented a process known as "IRP decoupling," through which Section 236 owners may prepay their mortgages but continue to receive IRPs. Owners must agree to maintain the affordability of the property for five years beyond the time period in which they receive the IRPs.[123] Owners may continue to receive IRPs either through the balance of the term of the original Section 236 mortgage or longer if the owner requests it; however, if the term of IRPs is lengthened, then the amount of each IRP is reduced.[124]

Flexible Subsidy Program

By the late 1970s, some assisted housing properties were facing financial distress and risking default on their HUD-assisted financing. If the properties defaulted, the federal government would face financial losses through FHA as well as the loss of affordable housing units. In response, Congress created a new Operating Assistance for Troubled Multifamily Housing Properties program as part of the Housing and Community Development Amendments of 1978 (P.L. 95-557). The program was designed to "restore or maintain the financial soundness, assist in the improvement of the management, and to maintain the low- to moderate-income character" of certain assisted multifamily housing properties. The assistance was later expanded to include loans for capital improvements. Initially, projects assisted under the Section 236 IRP program, the Section 221(d)(3) BMIR program, and the Rent Supplement program were eligible to receive the assistance. Later, Congress expanded eligibility to certain Section 8 properties (those that were converted from RAP or Rent Supplement) and Section 202 properties, among others.[125] While the program was initially funded with appropriations, a revolving fund—the Flexible Subsidy Fund— was established later to provide assistance. This fund consisted of Section 236 excess residual receipts, as well as proceeds from loan repayments and interest.[126]

HUD provided Flexible Subsidy assistance through two programs. The Operating Assistance Program (OAP) provided temporary funding to replenish project reserves, cover operating costs, and pay for limited physical improvements. The assistance was provided as a non-amortizing "contingent loan" that could be repaid with excess residual receipts or upon the sale of the property. The Capital Improvement Loan Program (CILP) provided assistance intended to cover the cost of major capital improvements that could not be accomplished with program reserves. The assistance was provided in the form of amortizing loans, generally with an interest rate of 6%.[127] Properties that received Flexible Subsidy assistance were required to maintain affordability for the life of their original mortgage.[128]

New obligation authority for Flexible Subsidy assistance was last provided in FY1995. According to HUD, the Flexible Subsidy program was no longer needed after Congress created the authority for assistance through the Multifamily Assisted Housing Reform and Accountability Act (described in the next section of this report).[129]

RENTAL ASSISTANCE

Section 8 Expiring Contracts, Renewals, and the Multifamily Assisted Housing Reform and Accountability Act (MAHRA)

Both ELIHPA and LIHPRHA were primarily focused on the stock of housing eligible for mortgage prepayment; neither law addressed another threat to the assisted housing stock identified in the 1987 Preservation Task Force report: the cost of renewing project-based rental-assistance contracts. Most Section 8 contracts—which were originated between 1974 and 1983—had terms of 20 years and were funded with up-front appropriations. By the mid-1990s, the contracts had begun expiring. Renewing the contracts would require new budget authority, for which Congress would have to provide new appropriations. In a tight budget environment, there was a concern that the cost of renewing Section 8 contracts could take up an expanding share of the HUD budget, leading to less funding for other priorities. Not renewing the contracts would save money, but it would mean that low-income families would lose their housing assistance. Further complicating matters, many of these properties were FHA-insured and many were receiving above-market rents. If the owners faced a drop in rent as a result of the loss of assistance, they could end up in default on their loans and the federal government—through the FHA insurance fund—would face a financial loss. Congress also discovered that many of these FHA-insured and rent-assisted properties were financially or physically distressed, including a number that were being mismanaged.[130]

The policy problem facing Congress was how to restructure the program in a way that would be beneficial to the families living in these properties, cost-saving for the federal government, and attractive to project owners. Ultimately, Congress designed a restructuring program that reduced the federal subsidies to owners of properties insured by FHA, lowered the above-market rents payable to these owners, and restructured the mortgages of properties so that owners could operate effectively on less income.

This restructuring plan—referred to as Mark-to-Market—was created by the Multifamily Assisted Housing Reform and Affordability Act. It was passed by Congress as Title V of the VA-HUD Appropriations Act for FY1998 (P.L. 105-65). The act was signed into law on October 27, 1997, and it expired on September 30, 2001. The program was reauthorized through a series of continuing resolutions until January 10, 2002, when it was amended and reauthorized through FY2006 under Title VI of the Labor, Health and Human Services, Education, and Related Agencies Appropriations Act for FY2002

(P.L. 107-116).[131] Section 21043 of the Revised Continuing Appropriations Resolution, 2007 (P.L. 110-5) extended the authorization through October 1, 2011.[132]

Mark-to-Market and Section 8 Renewal

Ultimately, at the end of a Section 8 contract an owner has two options: renew the contract, or opt out of renewing the contract. Under the terms of MAHRA, as implemented by HUD, owners wishing to renew their Section 8 contracts face different renewal procedures depending on the circumstances of the property. Those circumstances include the original subsidy type, the type of property owner, the property's rents relative to market, and the financial state of the property. The owner generally has six options: renew at existing rents (if rents are at market), be referred for renewal through a full Mark-to-Market restructuring (if rents are above market), renew at higher rents (if rents are below market), renew subject to special rules (if exempted from restructuring), renew based on terms of earlier preservation initiatives, or opt-out of the program by not renewing. These processes are detailed in the Section 8 Renewal Policy Guidebook,[133] and are generally summarized below.

Mark-to-Market

The Mark-to-Market restructuring process is targeted to FHA-insured properties owned by for-profit owners receiving above-market rents. Owners of such properties with contracts up for renewal are referred to the Office of Affordable Housing Programs at HUD to be evaluated for Mark-to-Market eligibility. The Mark-to-Market process is designed to reduce rents to market rates. Owners participating in Mark-to-Market have two options: they can either accept the reduced rents and renew for a one-year term (referred to as Mark-to-Market "lite"); or they can accept the reduced rents and have their outstanding debt restructured (referred to as "full").

In a Mark-to-Market full restructuring, the owner's debt and income is renegotiated so that the income the owner receives is sufficient to cover rehabilitation needs, operating expenses, and reserve replenishment.[134] This is accomplished through a full or partial payment of claim from the FHA insurance fund.[135] The lower mortgage debt level can then be supported with lower rents.[136] Mark-to-Market full renewals are subject to 30-year affordability restrictions, meaning that the owner must commit to maintain the property under a project-based contract (subject to the availability of appropriations) for 30 years. Owners undergoing a Mark-to-Market "lite" transaction are not subject to long-term affordability agreements. The new rents are adjusted each year using Annual Adjustment Factors (AAFs) published by HUD.

According to HUD, as of January 21, 2010, over 2,000 Section 8 properties had gone through full Mark-to-Market mortgage restructurings, and almost 800 properties had been through Market-to-Market "lite" transactions.[137]

Mark-up-to-Market

Mark-up-to-Market was created in 1999 to provide an incentive for owners of below-market properties in strong markets to renew their contracts at market-comparable rents.[138] In order to be eligible, properties must be owned by for-profit or limited-distribution owners, they must be in good physical condition, and if the property has an affordability restriction, the owner must be able to terminate it without prior HUD permission.[139] In exchange for higher rents, owners that choose to go through Mark-up-to-Market renewals must agree to contract terms of at least five years. During that time, rents are adjusted each year using HUD's published AAFs.

Exception Projects

Some properties are not eligible for Mark-to-Market or Mark-up-to-Market, even if their rents are above or below market. These properties include properties that are owned by nonprofits, that were financed with state or local funding in lieu of FHA mortgage insurance, that have Section 202 or rural housing loans (unless it was refinanced with an FHA-insured mortgage), that participate in the Section 8 Moderate Rehabilitation Single Room Occupancy program, or that otherwise do not have an FHA-insured mortgage.

Exception projects are renewed at rents that are the lesser of current rents plus the local Operating Cost Adjustment Factors (OCAFs) established by HUD, or the rent level needed to meet operating expenses. If the owner signs a multiyear contract, the rents can be set either via OCAF or based on the needs of their budget (referred to as budget-based rent increases).

Other Renewals

Some properties have rents at market levels or have rents below market but the owners choose not to participate in Mark-up-to-Market. In these cases, owners can submit a Rent Comparability Study (RCS) and have their rents renewed at their current level, plus an OCAF adjustment or a budget-based rent increase. Unlike in Mark-up-to-Market cases, owners renewing under this option are not required to commit to five-year renewals or use agreements.[140]

Opt Out

If an owner chooses not to renew an expiring Section 8 contract, he or she is considered to be "opting-out."[141] Owners who opt out are subject to federal notification requirements and must notify tenants and HUD at least one year before the end of the contract of their intention to renew or not renew. Then, four months before contract termination, owners must formally notify HUD in writing if they are going to renew or opt out.

As noted earlier, tenants living in properties whose owners "opt out" are eligible for enhanced vouchers (see "Implications for Tenants" earlier in this report). Enhanced vouchers are tenant-based Section 8 vouchers with special attributes. Their values can increase to the gross rent for the unit, as long as it is reasonable, even if it exceeds local standards. Families must continue to contribute at least as much toward rent as they were before they received their voucher, even if it was above 30% of their income. And tenants who receive enhanced vouchers have the right to remain in their units as long as the units continue to be offered as rental housing, and as long as the tenants are in compliance with their leases (and state and local law).

Recent Initiatives: Contract Preservation Provisions and Green Retrofit Funding

Contract Preservation Provisions

In recent years, Congress has adopted two new preservation policies through the annual appropriations process, beginning with the FY2006 HUD appropriations law (P.L. 109-115). The first addresses HUD's treatment of HUD-owned or managed properties with Section 8 project-based rental assistance contracts. Section 311 of P.L. 109-115 required HUD, to the extent feasible, to maintain Section 8 project-based rental assistance contracts when managing or disposing of multifamily properties owned or held by the Secretary as a result of foreclosure. Prior practice had often been to terminate Section 8 project-based contracts and replace the assistance with vouchers. In cases where the Secretary determined that continued rental assistance payments for the existing property were not feasible, the provision permitted HUD to transfer the rental assistance to another multifamily property or replace it with vouchers.

The second policy permits HUD to approve the transfer of rental assistance contracts and use restrictions from one property to another under certain circumstances. Section 318 of P.L. 109-115 authorized the Secretary to approve the transfer of mortgage debt, project-based rental assistance, and use restrictions from one HUD-assisted multifamily housing property to another property in cases where the transferring property is either physically obsolete or economically nonviable. In order to approve the transfer, among other requirements, the receiving project must exceed physical standards and the Secretary must determine that the transfer is in the best interests of the tenants.

Because these authorities were provided through an appropriations act, they expire at the end of the fiscal year unless they are renewed. The FY2007 year-long continuing resolution (P.L. 110-5) extended the two preservation-related provisions through FY2007, and the FY2008 appropriations law (P.L. 110-161, Sections 220 and 215) made changes to the transfer authority and extended both provisions through the end of FY2008. The authorities have subsequently been extended in FY2009 and FY2010.[142] According to HUD, as of March 2010, the transfer authority has been used less than a dozen times since it was created in 2006.[143]

Green Retrofit Program for Multifamily Housing

The American Recovery and Reinvestment Act of 2009 (ARRA, P.L. 111-5) provided $250 million to fund retrofit investments in HUD-assisted multifamily properties that will reduce ongoing utility consumption, benefit resident health, and/or benefit the environment. HUD used the funding to create the Green Retrofit Program (GRP). Through GRP, HUD provided competitive grants and loans to owners of properties assisted through the Section 8 project-based rental assistance program, as well as the Section 202 and 811 programs. Owners receiving GRP funds are required to extend their affordability agreements for an additional 15 years.[144]

"At Risk" Properties

Discussions around the issue of affordable housing preservation assume that properties are at risk of being lost to the affordable housing stock, whether through mortgage prepayment, expiring contracts, or the financial or physical health of the property, unless there is some kind of intervention. However, not all properties present the same level or type of risk, and situations vary based on numerous factors, including existing subsidy structures, the condition of the property, the type of ownership, and the property location.[145]

For example, some assisted properties may not be at risk of being lost to the affordable housing stock at all. Mission-oriented owners of properties in good financial and physical condition may be likely to extend affordability agreements and may have little motivation to convert their properties to another use. In other cases, assisted properties may not be immediately at risk, but they may be in the future. For example, some properties have owners who would like to use the property for other purposes, but they are bound by extended affordability agreements. Other owners may wish to leave the affordable housing business, but cannot find a purchaser willing to pay the asking price for the property or commit to the long-term affordability agreements. Other owners may wish to sell, but they face economic disincentives, such as large capital gains taxes.

Some properties are more immediately at risk. Where properties face financial or physical distress, the owner may wish to maintain the property as affordable housing, but the income and subsidy structure may render the property unsustainable. And some properties are at risk because the owners have other, more desirable options at the end of their affordability restrictions. For example, a for-profit owner may have the option to profit from higher rents at the end of the affordability restriction.[146] Or a mission-oriented owner, such as a church, may decide that it would rather use its property for another mission-related purpose, such as a school or other facility, at the end of the affordability restriction.

In these various circumstances, different interventions may be necessary to preserve the properties as affordable housing, and those interventions could be costly. Given limits to federal resources, priorities may need to be established when determining whether and how to preserve affordable housing. The next section of the report discusses some of these priorities.

PRESERVATION PRIORITIES

An initial question in discussing preservation is whether the government should intervene to maintain federally assisted housing beyond its original contract term at all. The modes of subsidy that led to the creation of these properties—subsidized multifamily mortgages and project-based rental-assistance contracts—have been replaced with different models of assistance, such as the Section 8 tenant-based voucher program and the Low-Income Housing Tax Credit. The original HUD subsidy programs were ended, in part, because of their perceived limitations, particularly their high costs[147] and concerns that they concentrated poverty.

Today, Section 8 housing vouchers have become the primary form of deeply targeted housing assistance; there have even been proposals to replace the stock of federally assisted housing with vouchers.[148] Vouchers are considered less expensive than project-based assistance and provide families with mobility and housing choices. However, the voucher program has its limitations. Landlords are not required to accept vouchers, and for some populations, especially persons who are elderly or have disabilities, accessible housing may not be available in the private market.

These critiques of the voucher program are used to support calls for the preservation and development of project-based housing assistance.[149] With few exceptions,[150] no statutory authority exists to create new, deeply targeted HUD-assisted housing. The Low-Income Housing Tax Credit, and, to a lesser degree, the HOME Investment Partnerships Block Grant program, help to fund the creation of new affordable housing developments; however, they are not as deeply subsidized as the older, HUD rent-assisted properties. Given the limited funding and authority for developing new, deeply subsidized housing, the stock of federally assisted housing is currently irreplaceable. Further, in many cases, it would be more expensive to build new housing than it would be to preserve the existing stock.[151]

As evidenced by the history of federal housing preservation policy discussed earlier in this report, Congress and the federal government have generally taken the position that preserving assisted housing is a desirable federal housing policy goal.

However, even if it is less expensive than new construction, preservation can be costly. Many properties were built in the 1960s and 1970s and may be in need of repair in order to be habitable for an additional 20 to 40 years. As a result, funds are often needed for rehabilitation and improvements, possibly requiring federal grants or insured loans. Another cost could be funds for ongoing or new rental assistance. In cases where units already receive rental assistance (principally through Section 8), continued rental assistance is needed to maintain affordability for low-income tenants. In addition, some currently unassisted units may need rental assistance to help pay for increased operating costs after rehabilitation has occurred. A third possible cost may be providing incentives to owners to encourage them to maintain affordability or to sell to a purchaser who will.

In addition to the costs of preservation, a transaction may require the cooperation of multiple parties—building owners, tenants, the local community, and HUD—each of whom could have their own interest in whether and how a property is preserved. In addition, each property may have characteristics that make its preservation more or less costly and feasible. These characteristics can include the property location, its physical condition, the needs of the tenants, and the type of owner organization (nonprofit versus for-profit), together with the effectiveness of the owner. These factors, in turn, can create different options for owners, present the federal government with varying preservation costs, and affect community interest in maintaining the property as affordable housing.

This section of the report discusses several of the factors that may play a part in the decision to preserve federally assisted housing: property location, property condition, tenant needs, and type of owner. Given the reality of limited federal resources, HUD and Congress may have to weigh competing priorities to determine which preservation strategies are the most cost effective and which properties should be preserved.

Location and Community

The location of a property can affect its value, both positively and negatively. A well-located property may have many potential benefits for tenants, making its preservation a priority. For example, some assisted housing properties are located in desirable areas near public transportation or other community assets such as parks, schools, shops, medical providers, and community and senior centers. Access to public transportation may make it easier for low-income families to find and maintain employment or for families with special needs (such as those that include persons who are elderly or have disabilities) to be able to live independently. An assisted property might also be the only affordable rental housing in an otherwise low-poverty neighborhood. If it were no longer available, families may be required to move from an area of economic opportunity to one of concentrated poverty. In rural areas, an assisted housing property might be the only affordable housing available, or perhaps even the only rental housing available. At the same time, however, owners of properties that are desirably located may have an incentive to convert the property to a more profitable use when affordability restrictions end, making it difficult for potentially displaced families to find comparable housing.

Conversely, other federally assisted properties are located in areas with high concentrations of poverty and crime and with limited access to reliable public transportation and other community amenities.[152] These properties may serve to limit the opportunities of their tenants. Preserving well-located properties may be a higher priority than preserving properties in distressed areas with limited opportunities.

PHYSICAL CONDITION OF THE PROPERTY

The physical condition of an assisted property can also affect the feasibility of its preservation. Some properties have deteriorated to the point that they have difficulty passing annual housing quality inspections. It may be very expensive to repair these properties so that they can provide adequate housing for families. There can be many reasons that a property has fallen into physical disrepair, and those reasons may influence the cost and feasibility of its preservation.

Most physically distressed properties are also financially distressed. They have operating income that is low or negative, leading to underinvestment in routine maintenance and replacement reserves. These properties may be financially distressed because they were not designed in ways that would allow them to succeed. For example, demand for efficiency units is low, making it hard for properties featuring only efficiency units to compete with other properties, even in a subsidized market.[153] If a property's units are not desirable or well matched to demand in the surrounding community, it could have occupancy problems. High vacancy rates can lead to financial distress, which can ultimately lead to physical decline.

While some owners may be unwilling or unable to maintain properties, in some cases a property may be physically well designed and desirable, but the financing and/or subsidy structure has led to a financial imbalance. For example, many for-profit property owners took accelerated depreciation and mortgage interest tax deductions early in their property ownership. This allowed them to have strong and positive cash flow. But, over time, if the owner was unable to recapitalize the property (secure new funding for improvements),[154] those deductions became unavailable, leaving the owner with insufficient income to cover operating expenses, replacement reserves, and tax liability later. This may be due to poor planning on the part of the owner, or to changing market conditions.

Whether or not a physically distressed property is worth preserving may depend on the level of deterioration, the overall relevance and desirability of the design of the property, and other factors.

TENANT NEEDS

The needs of a tenant population may make preservation a priority in some cases, principally in the case of elderly tenants and tenants with disabilities. When the alternative to preservation is providing tenants with Section 8 vouchers, tenants who are elderly or have a disability may have difficulty finding housing that meets their needs, particularly if their mobility is impaired. The difficulty of relocating, combined with potential accessibility features of HUD-assisted properties, could weigh in favor of preservation. In addition, some properties offer supportive services through a service coordinator or other means; if those properties are not preserved, tenants may not be able to find replacement housing where services are offered.

According to CRS analysis of resident characteristics data from HUD, about 62% of families living in HUD rent-assisted properties were elderly and/or disabled.[155]

TYPE OF OWNER

The characteristics of property owners may affect their willingness or ability to maintain affordability after their contracts with HUD expire. Profit-motivated owners may be more likely to sell their property or convert it to market-rate housing than mission-driven, nonprofit organizations. In 2006, HUD released an analysis of properties that had left HUD programs, comparing their characteristics to those properties that remained part of the assisted housing stock. Of those owners that either prepaid their mortgages or opted out of Section 8 contracts, 86% were for-profit organizations (compared to 55% of total owners that were for-profit) while only 9% were nonprofits.[156] HUD commented on the fact that nonprofit owners have been less likely to leave HUD-assisted housing: "many nonprofits are motivated by the goal of providing affordable housing to low-income people, and would not opt out even if they could leave the stock."[157] Properties with for-profit owners may require more costly preservation incentives than those with nonprofit owners.

Another factor could be an owner's ability to operate and maintain the property. If an owner has not operated a property well or has allowed it to deteriorate, HUD may not be willing to continue subsidies or extend preservation incentives to the existing owner.

WEIGHING THE COSTS AND BENEFITS OF PRESERVATION

Weighing the costs and benefits of preserving an assisted housing property can be difficult. This is due, at least in part, to the wide range of stakeholders in the property. For any given property, the stakeholders include the property owner, the tenants, the surrounding neighborhood, the state and local government, the federal government (specifically HUD), and, potentially, Members of Congress. These stakeholders may have different views about the relative costs and benefits of preserving the property.

- Owners are generally focused on maximizing their financial investments, although nonprofit owners may have mission-oriented goals (which may or may not involve affordable housing).
- Residents' concerns could include preventing their own displacement or improving their own living environments; however, thoughts about the best way to achieve either goal could vary from resident to resident.
- Local community leaders, and local and/or state government officials, could see the property as a valuable community asset, or as a blight and a tax on local resources.
- Similarly, HUD may see the property as a high-performing federal asset, or as a low-performing risk to the FHA insurance fund.

Some Members of Congress may consider it important to preserve existing subsidies due to limited authority to create new project-based housing, but other Members may see the cost of preservation as being too high given their desire to limit discretionary spending.

The heterogeneity of the assisted housing stock further complicates efforts to consider the costs and benefits of preservation. As outlined earlier, some properties are better located than others, some are in better physical conditions than others, some serve particularly vulnerable populations, and their owners have varying levels of commitment and capacity. The subsidy status of the properties also varies widely. Some have received relatively large amounts of federal funding over the years through rental-assistance contracts and subsidized mortgages; others have received much less, perhaps only an interest rate that was initially below market, but is now at or above market. These factors influence both the potential cost of preserving the property as well as the potential implications of not acting to preserve the property.

Ultimately, when it comes to assisted housing preservation, owners can choose what to do with their properties. However, these choices are constrained by federal, state, or local laws and may be influenced by the availability of preservation incentives. For example, as described earlier, property owners cannot terminate rental-assistance contracts without first providing at least one year's notification to tenants. This policy is designed to give tenants time to organize an attempt to launch a preservation effort, or to prepare for a change in their subsidy status. In terms of incentives, HUD has historically held the primary role in determining which properties have access to preservation incentives, although the agency may take into account the views of other stakeholders.

PROPERTY CHARACTERISTICS

As noted earlier, there are several different types of assisted housing properties at issue in terms of preservation. Some have assisted financing (through FHA or the Section 202 loan program), some have rental-assistance contracts, and some have both. The level of affordability of the property, the length of time the affordability must be maintained, and the options at the end of the assistance contract all vary depending on the type of subsidy provided. This section of the report presents detailed characteristics of properties at issue in preservation, organized around types of assistance. The first section presents data regarding the Section 202 loan program, the second section covers the Section 236 and Section 221(d)(3) BMIR programs, and the third section presents data regarding units receiving rental assistance through the Rent Supplement, RAP, and sections. For example, *Table 1* includes Section 202 units that receive rental assistance; these units are also included in *Table 7,* which shows all rent-assisted units. See *Table A-1* in *Appendix A* for disaggregated units.

Section 202 Loans

As can be seen in *Table 1*, there are 2,786 properties with active Section 202 loans. The majority of units in those properties receive rental assistance.

As discussed previously, HUD inspects properties annually, biannually, or every three years, depending on the property's most recent inspection score. Under HUD regulations, properties with scores below 30 are automatically referred to the Departmental Enforcement Center (DEC) for corrective action, and recently, HUD has adopted a policy that properties with scores above 30 but below 60 should also be referred, unless there are mitigating circumstances.[158]

Properties in poor physical condition are at risk of default on their HUD assistance contracts and of being lost to the affordable housing stock. Less than 3% of properties with Section 202 loans have scores low enough to require referral to the Departmental Enforcement Center, and more than 60% have inspection scores high enough to require inspection only every three years.

Table 1. Properties and Units with Active Section 202 Loans

	Properties	Units	Rent Assisted Units	Persent assisted
Active section 202 Loans	2,786	144.506	118.428	82%

Source: CRS analysis of HUD data from the Multifamily Assistance and Section 8 Contracts Database and the 202 Direct Loans database, as of September 30, 2009.

Table 2. Loan Maturity Date Ranges for Properties with Active 202 Loans

Maturity Dates	Properties	Unassisted Units	Assisted Units	Total Units
Through 2014	47	3.354	1.342	4.696
2015-2019	183	9.789	12.619	22.408
2020-2024	979	9.672	53.076	62.748
2025-beyond	1.567	3.045	51.205	54.250

Source: CRS analysis of HUD data from the Multifamily Assistance and Section 8 Contracts Database and the 202 Direct Loans database, as of September 30, 2009.

Note: Ten properties were missing maturity dates.

Table 3. REAC Inspection Scores for Properties with Active 202 Loans

REAC Scores	Number of Properties	Percent of Properties
30 or below, automatic referral to DEC	4	0.1%
31-59, referral to DEC	73	2.6%
60-79, annual inspections	310	11.2%
80-89, biennial inspections	656	23.6%
90 and above, inspections every three years	1.737	62.5%

Source: CRS analysis of HUD data from the 202 Direct Loans database and the Multifamily Assisted Property Physical Inspection Dataset, as of September 30, 2009 .

Note: Six properties were missing inspection scores.

Financing Assistance: Rent-Restricted, Insured Units

As shown in *Table 4,* there are about 1,542 properties with mortgage insurance through the Section 236 and Section 221d(3) BMIR programs. As discussed earlier in this report, these mortgage insurance programs conferred affordability restrictions on the properties and their owners. The properties with active Section 236 or BMIR financing provide more than 170,000 units of housing subject to affordability restrictions; about 56% of those units also have rental assistance.

Table 4. Active Section 236 and BMIR Properties and Units

	Properties	Total Units	Rent-Assisted Units	Percent Rent-Assisted Units
Active Section 236 and BMIR Financing	1,542	170.667	95.532	56%

Source: CRS analysis of HUD data from the Multifamily Assistance and Section 8 Contracts Database and the Insured Multifamily Mortgages Database, as of September 30, 2009.

Note: Data extracted from the Insured Multifamily Mortgages Database based on "Section of Act" identification codes provided to CRS by HUD.

Table 5. Mortgage Maturity Date Ranges for Active 236 and BMIR Properties

Maturity Periods	Properties	Unassisted Units	Rent-Assisted Units	Total Units
through 2014	1,145	57,835	65,500	123,335
2015-2019	317	14,249	24,066	38,315
2020-2024	18	1,361	1,329	2,690
2025-beyond	62	1,690	4,637	6,327

Source: CRS analysis of HUD data from the Multifamily Assistance and Section 8 Contracts Database and the Insured Multifamily Mortgages Database, as of September 30, 2009.

Table 6. Inspection Scores for Active 236 and BMIR Properties with Rental Assistance

Inspection Scores	Number of Properties	Percent of Properties
30 or below, automatic referral to DEC	10	0.8%
31-59, referral to DEC	71	5.8%
60-79, annual inspections	202	16.5%
80-89, biennial inspections	382	31.2%
90 and above, inspections every three years	561	45.8%

Source: CRS analysis of HUD data from the Multifamily Assisted Property Physical Inspection Dataset Database, the Insured Multifamily Mortgages Database, and the Section 8 Contracts Database, as of September 30, 2009.

Note: CRS was unable to include inspection scores for Section 236 and BMIR properties that do not receive rental assistance due to data limitations.

As discussed earlier in this report, upon maturation of Section 236 and BMIR insured loans, owners have the authority to convert their properties to market uses, including charging market-rate rents. Upon such a conversion, any units with rental assistance will continue to receive rent assistance under the terms of the rent-assistance contract while it is in effect. If the owner does not renew the rent-assistance contract, except in the case of units with Rent Supplement contracts, the residents will receive tenant protection vouchers, and in many cases, they will receive enhanced vouchers. Renters in unassisted properties are not eligible for tenant protection vouchers upon maturation under current law. As shown in *Table 5*, most of these properties are facing mortgage maturation in the next five years, with about 57,835 units at risk of unassisted rent increases.

As shown in *Table 6,* about 7% of FHA-insured, rent-restricted properties had inspection scores low enough to require referral to the Departmental Enforcement Center for corrective action. The highest percentage of properties (45.8%) have scores high enough to require inspections only every three years.

Rental Assistance

As shown in *Table 7*, there are 17,207 properties that have rental-assistance contracts with HUD. Note that in a given property, it is possible that some units are not covered by a rental-assistance contract. In aggregate, of the more than 1.4 million units in the rent-assisted properties, 88% are covered by rental-assistance contracts. It is also possible that a property can have contracts for more than one type of rental assistance. Most rent-assisted properties have only Section 8 assistance;[159] only about 2% of properties have only RAP assistance or Rent Supplement assistance. A small number of properties have a combination of the different types of rental assistance (for example, both a Section 8 and RAP contract). Not surprisingly, the percentage of units assisted in RAP-only and Rent Supplement-only properties is much lower than the percentage of units assisted in Section 8-only properties, since both the RAP and Rent Supplement programs had limits on the percentage of units that could be assisted in a property.

Including those units in properties with a mix of contracts, there are 15,870 RAP units, 12,847 Rent Supplement units, and 1.2 million Section 8 units. From a preservation standpoint, the type of assistance is important. HUD has no authority to renew RAP and Rent Supplement contracts, which assist nearly 30,000 units, and only has the authority to provide tenant protection vouchers upon contract termination to tenants in Rent Supplement units, not tenants in RAP units.

Table 8 provides information on the expiration period for rent-assistance contracts, broken down by type. As is shown in the table, most Rent Supplement expirations will happen within the next five years, whereas most RAP expirations will happen within the next 10 years. Under current law, these contracts cannot be renewed. Most Section 8 contracts will expire in the next five years. For the most part, owners can choose to renew Section 8 contracts if they wish.

Table 7. Rent-Assisted Properties and Units

	Total Properties	Total Units in Assisted Properties	Assisted Units	Percent Assisted
All rental assistance	17,207	1,405,606	1,233,426	88%
RAP contracts only	129	28,201	15,416	55%
Rent Supplement contracts only	242	38,754	12,311	32%
Section 8 contracts only	16,811	1,335,313	1,203,215	90%
Mix of rental-assistance contract types	25	3,338	2,484	74%

Table 8. Expirations for RAP and Rent Supplement Contracts

Contract Expirations	Section 8 Assisted Units	Rap Assisted Units	Rent Supplement Assisted Units	Total Assisted Units	Persent Assisted Units
through 2014	793,296	1,439	8,991	803,726	65%
2015-2019	91,122	13,933	3,750	108,805	9%
2020-2024	181,154	401	76	181,631	15%
2025-beyond	139,132	97	30	139,259	11%

Source: CRS analysis of HUD data from the Multifamily Assistance and Section 8 Contracts Database, as of September 30, 2009.

As noted earlier in this report, the ownership type of a property can be indicative of the likelihood that the owner will choose to exit an assisted housing program. As shown in *Table 9*, approximately 41% of properties with rental-assistance contracts are owned by nonprofit owners.

Roughly 42% are owned by for-profit owners. Another 15% are owned by limited-dividend owners. Limited-dividend owners face caps on the return they can receive on their investment in a rent-assisted property. As a result, limited dividend may be the ownership type with the greatest incentive to leave the program, depending on other factors.

Another factor that can affect whether a property remains part of the assisted housing stock is the physical condition of the property. As can be seen in *Table 10*, the majority of properties with rent-assistance contracts have high enough inspection scores to allow them to be inspected only every three years. However, 6% of properties, at their last inspection, had scores low enough to require corrective action.

Table 9. Ownership of Rent-Assisted Properties

Ownership Types	Percent of Properties
Limited dividend	15%
Nonprofit	41%
Other	2%
For-Profit	42%

Source: CRS analysis of HUD data from the Multifamily Assistance and Section 8 Contracts Database, as of September 30, 2009.
Note: 1,947 properties had missing values for property ownership type.

Table 10. Inspection Scores for Rent-Assisted Properties at Latest Inspection

Inspection Scores	Number of Properties	Percent of Properties
30 or below, automatic referral to DEC	105	1%
31-59, referral to DEC	801	5%
60-79, annual inspections	2,479	14%
80-89, biennial inspections	4,686	27%
90 and above, inspections every three years	9,061	53%

Source: CRS analysis of HUD data from the Multifamily Assistance and Section 8 Contracts Database and the Multifamily Assisted Property Physical Inspection Dataset, as of September 30, 2009.
Note: 75 properties had missing values.

Summary

As presented in these data (including the data presented in *Table A-1* in *Appendix A*), almost 17,700 properties containing more than 1.33 million subsidized units (with financing or rental assistance) have some form of federal affordability restrictions that are scheduled to end.[160] In some cases, those agreements will be renewed and continued, in other cases, they will be terminated at the owner's choice, at HUD's choice, or because there is no authority to renew the agreements. Those in the latter category are the easiest to identify. Just under 29,000 units of housing are subsidized by RAP and Rent Supplement contracts that HUD has no authority to renew. More than 10,000 of those contracts will expire in the next five years. However, HUD does have authority to provide ongoing rental assistance, in the form of tenant protection vouchers, to those families living in units with expiring Rent Supplement contracts. These represent just under 13,000 total units, well over half of which will expire in the next five years. HUD does not have the authority to provide ongoing rental assistance to those families living in units with expiring RAP contracts; these represent more than 16,000 total units, of which just under 10% will expire in the next five years.

HUD also does not have any current tools to extend affordability agreements on properties with maturing HUD-assisted financing through the Section 202, Section 221(d)(3) BMIR, and Section 236 programs. While those properties with HUD-assisted financing together with Section 8 contracts can extend their federal affordability agreements through renewal of their Section 8 contracts, properties without Section 8 contracts do not have this option. There are 315 properties with FHA-insured loans through the Section 236 or Section 221(d)(3) BMIR programs containing over 31,000 units, and 176 properties with Section 202 loans containing just under 15,000 units that have no rental-assistance contracts. While some of these owners may not increase their rents to market rates once the affordability restrictions end, there is no federal law preventing them from doing so and there is no federal rent assistance available to the families living in these units if their rents increase.

For those properties that have the option to extend their affordability agreements, it can be difficult to determine what may happen at the end of their current agreements. Of the more than 1.2 million units with Section 8 assistance that can be renewed, over half have rental-assistance contracts that will expire over the next five years. As long as the property is not in default of its assistance contract (and, as shown in *Table 10*, most properties have at least passing physical inspection scores), the owner can decide whether or not to renew the contract. Well over half of these rent-assisted properties are owned by for-profit entities, including the 15% owned by for-profit owners who receive "limited-dividends," or caps on their profits. While all for-profit owners may be at greater risk of opting-out of renewing their contracts than nonprofit owners, limited-dividend owners may be the most likely not to renew if they can receive comparable rents, and greater profits, in the private market.

PRESERVATION OPTIONS

As described earlier in this report, the federal government has a limited set of preservation tools. HUD has the authority to renew expiring rental-assistance contracts for those properties that have them, and, in some circumstances, restructure the outstanding debt on a property if it has FHA-insured financing. In other circumstances, HUD has the authority to provide residents facing displacement with rental assistance. For properties with maturing mortgages, HUD has no preservation authority. Earlier preservation laws gave HUD additional tools, including the authority to provide new rental-assistance contracts, secondary financing to shore up troubled properties, and enhanced restrictions on property owners' rights to exit certain programs. These additional preservation tools are no longer available; they were eliminated out of concern about their high cost and about their infringement on property owners' rights.

In recent years, particularly as concern about maturing mortgages has grown, there have been calls from low-income housing advocates, tenants'-rights organizations, and property owners to adopt policies that encourage preservation and expand the set of preservation tools available to HUD. A number of proposals that would encourage housing preservation have been made as part of legislation[161] or through recommendations from interested groups.[162] These proposals generally fall into two broad categories: (1) incentives for current owners to maintain their properties or sell them to preservation purchasers, and (2) restrictions on owners.

It is important to note that federal efforts are not the only preservation efforts. In recent years, state and local governments, along with affordable housing preservation advocates, have increased the local role in affordable housing preservation. Several states and localities have set aside their own funds, or prioritized the use of their federal funds, for preservation incentives. For example, according to CRS analysis of 2008 state Low-Income Housing

Tax Credit (LIHTC) Qualified Allocation Plans, 27 states awarded additional points to preservation projects in their competitions for tax credits, and an additional 17 states set aside a portion of tax credits for preservation purposes.

The following section of the report discusses current federal preservation policy options.

Financial Incentives for the Current Owner to Maintain Affordability

There are a number of methods through which the government could provide incentives for existing owners to maintain their properties as affordable housing. These options include reducing owner debt, increasing the amount of rent subsidies owners receive, allowing owners to access reserve funds, or providing funds to rehabilitate and improve properties. One consideration when offering incentives is what strings to attach to them. Generally, when owners have received preservation incentives in the past they have been required to extend any affordability restrictions (for between five and 30 years, depending on the incentive) and, in some cases, renew any expiring rental-assistance contracts. Incentive options include the following:

- Debt reduction—Reducing owners' debt may reduce their operating costs, freeing up funds for needed repairs, or it may make it more feasible for owners to enter into new loans, the proceeds of which could be used to rehabilitate properties. HUD could be given explicit authority to subordinate or forgive loans that it made to property owners over the years. For example, HUD extended Flexible Subsidy loans to Section 236 and Section 202 owners, among others, to help "restore or maintain the financial or physical soundness of the project."163 If HUD waived this debt in the case of a refinancing, an owner would not have to use loan proceeds to pay off the debt and would have more funds available to improve the property. HUD could also be given authority to make partial payments of claim from the FHA insurance fund to reduce the debt of FHA-insured properties. HUD already has the authority to do this in certain circumstances; that authority is primarily used in Mark-to-Market transactions.
- Increased rents and/or rent assistance—If owners were to receive higher rents, they might be better able to pay for improvements to their properties or may be willing to continue to provide affordable

housing. In the case of rent-assisted units, the federal government would likely pay the cost of increased rents. In the case of units without rent assistance, lower-income tenants could end up paying the cost of increased rents unless additional rent subsidies were provided.

- Access to reserves—Some property owners with rental-assistance contracts are required to establish residual receipt accounts. In some circumstances, HUD can permit owners to access these funds for reinvestment in the property.[164] Expanding access to these reserves could give owners the incentive to maintain their properties as affordable housing.
- Loans or grants for recapitalization—HUD could make loans or grants directly to building owners to enable them to improve their properties. This has happened in the past through the Flexible Subsidy Program. Currently, HUD does not receive any funding for this purpose.

Incentives to Sell to Preservation Purchasers

Another method of preserving housing is to give owners incentives to sell their properties to organizations that will continue to maintain affordability for some period of time. This could occur with owners who no longer wish to participate as affordable housing providers or where owners are not considered "good" owners by the residents, the local community, and HUD. The potential buyers in this scenario are sometimes referred to as "preservation purchasers" and are often nonprofit organizations or state housing finance agencies, and, in some circumstances, organizations of residents. Incentives to sell to preservation purchasers could come in different forms:

- Exit tax relief—Congress could enact a law to reduce the tax liability of owners that sell their properties to preservation purchasers. Some for-profit owners face large tax bills when they sell their assisted properties due to capital gains taxes.[165] In cases where owners have held property for decades, capital gains taxes may be quite high and act as a disincentive for the owner to sell the property.
- Financial assistance for preservation purchasers—In some cases, potential preservation purchasers do not have the technical expertise or access to funding necessary to allow them to purchase a property. In order to aid preservation purchasers, federal funding could be used to provide technical assistance and/or pre-development grants that

would aid preservation purchasers in putting together financing to purchase a property. Funding could also be provided for direct grants or loans to help preservation entities purchase and rehabilitate a property. Another option is to fund additional rental-assistance contracts, which can serve to both provide ongoing operating assistance and act as a credit enhancement when a purchaser is seeking private market financing.

Requirements for Current Owners

Another way to preserve affordable housing would be to impose requirements on property owners. Such requirements could include limiting an owner's options in selling the property, giving tenants the right to enforce existing housing quality standards, and expanding tenant notification requirements.

An advantage of owners requirements is that they can accomplish the goal of preservation without costly incentives. However, requirements that restrict an owner's ability to sell or convert a property to market-rate housing could result in legal challenges. As discussed earlier in this report ("Previous and Ongoing Efforts to Preserve Assisted Housing"), in the late 1980s and early 1990s Congress enacted laws designed to limit the ability of owners to end affordability restrictions. The laws resulted in years of litigation over whether these restrictions resulted in a constitutional "takings" claim. The federal government has lost several of these lawsuits and some are still pending. Owner requirement options include the following:

- Right of first refusal or right of first purchase for preservation purchaser[166]—One proposal is to give preservation purchasers a right to purchase properties in order to prevent them from being converted to market-rate housing. In this scenario, if an owner wanted to sell the property he or she would first have to attempt to sell the property to an organization that would maintain affordability, or would have to accept a fair market offer by a preservation purchaser over other offers.
- Right of first refusal or right of first purchase for tenants—Another option similar to the right of first purchase or right of first refusal for a preservation purchaser would be offering the same rights to tenants. The idea is that, with sufficient notification, tenants can get technical

assistance, organize themselves, and purchase the property in which they live.

- Tenant enforcement of HUD contracts—A criticism preservation advocates have made of current policy is that tenants have no way to compel HUD to enforce its rules, such as those meant to ensure that properties do not deteriorate to the point that they fail inspection. It has been proposed that if tenants were given the standing to compel enforcement with contract rules, properties may be better maintained and may not be at risk of loss due to HUD enforcement action. This type of private right of action exists in fair housing law and would give tenants greater power in negotiation with private property owners.
- Tenant notification—In cases where owners plan to convert units to market-rate housing or sell the property to an owner that will not maintain affordability, they must notify tenants. Proposals have been made to expand these notification requirements; this would help resident groups organize in case they wish to purchase the property or contest a sale, or it would give them ample time to find alternative arrangements with their vouchers. Current law requires that owners give a minimum notification of at least 150 days before prepaying an FHA-insured mortgage and at least a one-year notice before choosing not to renew a Section 8 contract.

What if Property is Not Preserved?

In some cases, a property either cannot be preserved with existing incentives, or should not be preserved, perhaps due to its physical condition or location. In circumstances where an individual property will not be preserved, there may be options to either transfer the assistance to another property or provide residents with ongoing assistance.

- Transferring Section 8 assistance—If a property is significantly deteriorated, outdated, or poorly located, one preservation option is to transfer the assistance attached to the property (its rental-assistance contract and/or its affordability restriction) to another, better-suited property. The idea is to preserve the existing assistance, since there is no authority for new rental-assistance contracts or affordability restrictions. In recent years, Congress has given HUD limited authority to undertake these types of transfers,[167] and there has been interest in further expanding that authority.

- Expanded Enhanced Voucher Eligibility—In the case of mortgage prepayment or termination of a Section 8 contract, the tenants receive vouchers in some circumstances. These vouchers are designed to provide ongoing rent assistance to tenants and to protect them from rent increases, which may allow them to remain in their current rental units. In the case of the expiration of RAP and Rent Supplement contracts, as well as in the case of mortgage maturation or HUD-approved prepayments (in the absence of rental-assistance contracts), the residents are not eligible for vouchers. There have been proposals to expand enhanced voucher eligibility to those groups that are not currently eligible.

RECENT LEGISLATIVE INITIATIVES

Several preservation-related proposals were considered in the 111th Congress. One was enacted, the other may be considered again in the 112th Congress.

The Housing Preservation and Tenant Protection Act (H.R. 4868, 111th Congress)

An extensive preservation bill, the Housing Preservation and Tenant Protection Act (H.R. 4868) was introduced in the House on March 17, 2010, by the Chairman of the House Financial Services Committee. The bill was similar to a draft preservation bill that had been circulated as part of a hearing held by the Subcommittee on Housing and Community Opportunity of the House Financial Services Committee in July 2009.[168] The bill included versions of most of the proposals discussed in the previous section of this report. Among others, the bill included the following provisions:

- Regarding Section 221(d)(3) BMIR and Section 236 properties with maturing mortgages, H.R. 4868 would have authorized HUD to make grants or loans available to rehabilitate the property if owners so chose, and would have extended enhanced voucher protections to unassisted tenants upon mortgage maturation. The bill would also have created a "Preservation Exchange Program," through which HUD could facilitate the transfer of a property with a maturing mortgage to a preservation purchaser. The bill would have authorized HUD to provide incentives both to current owners and purchasers, including the forgiveness of outstanding Flexible Subsidy loans.

- H.R. 4868 would have authorized the conversion of RAP and Rent Supplement contracts to Section 8, which would allow them to be renewed and would have expanded certain owners' access to their residual receipts accounts.
- The bill would have established a form of right of first refusal/right of first purchase for HUD (or its assignee) whereby HUD could match the offer of a third party and purchase a property in order to maintain its affordability.
- H.R. 4868 would have permitted owners to request project-based assistance in lieu of enhanced vouchers, and would have required HUD to provide such assistance, as long as the owner agreed to extend the contract at least 20 years.
- In terms of tenant protection and assistance, H.R. 4868 would have authorized funding for technical assistance for tenant organizations and given tenants a private right of action to enforce program rules.
- The bill also contained a version of the Section 202 preservation legislation (discussed in the next section of this report), as well as an authorization and modification to rural housing preservation initiatives that have been authorized and funded through recent appropriations acts.

The legislation would have authorized "such sums as necessary" to fund various preservation incentives, making it dependent on the Appropriations Committees to fund most of the new initiatives.

Both low-income housing advocates and industry organizations representing assisted property owners provided feedback on the draft legislation during the hearings in 2009.[169] While many of the proposals contained in the draft legislation were supported by both advocates and owners groups, provisions related to restrictions on owners (right of first purchase/right of first refusal and private right of standing for residents) proved controversial, with tenant advocates in support of the provisions and owners groups opposed. Based on testimony given during a hearing on the introduced legislation on March 24, 2010,[170] property owners continued to be concerned about the right of first refusal and private right of standing provisions and tenant advocates continue to support such provisions.

The bill was marked up and approved by the House Financial Services Committee in July, 2010; however, it was not considered on the House floor before the end of the 111th Congress.

The Section 202 Supportive Housing for the Elderly Act (S. 118)

In December 2010, both the Senate and the House passed the Section 202 Supportive Housing for the Elderly Act (S. 118), a law that gives owners of older Section 202 developments the ability to refinance, improve, and potentially preserve their properties, and that also extends the term of affordability in cases of refinancing. Many of the housing developments built during the loan phase of the Section 202 program (from approximately 1959 to 1990) are getting older and may be in need of repair and modernization. One way in which property owners may obtain funds for improving their properties is by refinancing their original Section 202 loans. Some of the older buildings may have a good deal of equity available, and owners may also be in a position to take advantage of lower interest rates. Under the law prior to the enactment of S. 118, owners could refinance their Section 202 loans if the refinancing resulted "in a lower interest rate on the principal of the loan for the project and in reductions in debt service" (i.e., reduced principal and interest payments).[171] However, because loans extended prior to 1974 have interest rates of about 3%, it was difficult, if not impossible, to refinance into a loan with reduced debt service. Under S. 118, loans with interest rates at or below 6% can be refinanced without the requirement of lower debt service as long as owners use the proceeds to address the property's physical needs.[172]

The law also outlines the ways in which owners are able to use proceeds from a refinancing. Previous law described how savings that result from a refinancing could be used for various purposes and required that at least 50% be used in a manner that is advantageous to tenants. S. 118 amended this section of the law. While S. 118 continues to allow owners to use proceeds from a refinancing in a manner that is advantageous to tenants, it also allows owners to use proceeds to provide affordable rental housing and social services for elderly persons living in another HUD-assisted property owned by the same entity. New purposes for which owners can use refinancing proceeds under S. 118 include 15% for supportive services, or more with a waiver from HUD (current law does not allow for HUD waivers), and payment of developers' fees.

In addition, S. 118 extends the term of affordability to 20 years beyond the term of the original Section 202 loan. Previously, owners who refinanced were required to maintain affordability only through the term of the original Section 202 loan. Another change to existing law contained in S. 118 is a new "preservation project rental assistance" program, which will be available to owners who refinance their Section 202 loans in order to prevent displacement of tenants. Not all Section 202 units receive rental assistance, particularly those financed prior to 1974,[173] and if owners have to increase rents due to increased debt service, the rental assistance may prevent displacement of tenants.

Appendix A. Preservation Properties at a Glance

Table A-1. Categories of Preservation Properties

Property Type	Level of Affordability	Length of Affordability	Type of Participating Owners	Type of Families Served	Options at the End of Assistance Contract	Approximate Number of Properties (Units)
FHA Mortgage Insurance Only (No rental assistance)	In the Section 236 program, residents pay basic rent (the amount the owners need to support the facilities at a 1% mortgage interest rate) or 30% of their income. In the Section 21(d)(3) BMIR program, tenants pay the BMIR rent as set by HUD.	Initial contracts were for 40 years; however, private for-profit owners were given the option of prepaying their mortgages and ending use restrictions after 20 years.	Owners may be nonprofit or for-profit entities.	For Section 236 properties, eligible households are those earning 80% or less of the area median income (AMI), and for Section 221(d)(3) properties, income eligibility is set at 95% of AMI (although owners may admit over-income tenants in certain circumstances in both programs).	At prepayment or default, residents receive Section 8 vouchers. At maturation, owners can raise rents to market rate and there is no authority for vouchers.	315 properties (31,532 total units)

Table A-1. (Continued).

Property Type	Level of Affordability	Length of Affordability	Type of Participating Owners	Type of Families Served	Options at the End of Assistance Contract	Approximate Number of Properties (Units) [a]
Rental Assistance [b] Only [c] (No BMIR, 236, 202)	Residents pay 30% of their incomes toward rent.	Initial contracts could be up to 20 years; renewal contracts are generally for five year terms, although they can be for 20 year terms depending on the renewal option.	Owners may be nonprofit or for-profit entities.	Tenants are low-income, with most assistance targeted to very low-income and extremely low-income tenants.	Owner can choose to renew contract under one of several options. If owner chooses not to renew, then tenants receive vouchers.	13,370 properties (1,136,783 total units; 1,019,466 rent-assisted units)
FHA Mortgage Insurance with Rental Assistance	Residents in assisted units pay 30% of their incomes toward rent; unassisted renters pay either basic rents (Section 236) or the BMIR rent (Section 221(d)(3) BMIR).	Generally, the longer of the mortgage insurance use restriction or the rental-assistance contract.	Owners may be nonprofit or for-profit entities.	Families must be low-income in order to reside in units with rental assistance. Families living in unassisted units must meet the income requirements of the mortgage insurance	At prepayment or default, all residents in properties with Section 8 contracts receive vouchers. Upon mortgage maturation, rents can go to	1,227 properties (139,135 total units; 95,532 rent-assisted units)

Property Type	Level of Affordability	Length of Affordability	Type of Participating Owners	Type of Families Served	Options at the End of Assistance Contract	Approximate Number of Properties (Units) [a]
				program.	market rate. HUD does not have the authority to renew RAP and Rent Supplement contracts upon expiration.	
Section 202 Loan Only	Rent set by owner based on funds required to support building operating expenses.	During the 1960s, loan terms were 50 years; the term was reduced to 40 years as part of the Housing and Community Development Act of 1974.	Owners must be nonprofit organizations.	Tenants are either elderly families (those with a member age 62 or older) or tenants with disabilities. Unassisted units are generally meant to be affordable to low- or moderate-income households.	Owners must maintain affordability through the term of the original mortgage, even in cases of prepayment. After the mortgage expires, owners may increase rents to market rate and tenants do not receive vouchers.	176 properties (14,699 total units)

Table A-1. (Continued).

Property Type	Level of Affordability	Length of Affordability	Type of Participating Owners	Type of Families Served	Options at the End of Assistance Contract	Approximate Number of Properties (Units)
Section 202 Loan with Rental Assistance	In assisted units, residents pay 30% of their income toward rent. In unassisted units, tenants pay rent set by owner.	The restrictions due to loan terms are 40 years, with initial Section 8 contract terms up to 20 years.	Owners must be nonprofit organizations	Elderly tenants and tenants with disabilities living in assisted units must be low-income.	Owners must maintain affordability under the terms of the loan and rental-assistance contracts even in cases of prepayment. If the mortgage matures, rents can be increased to market and only Section 8 assisted residents receive vouchers.	2,610 properties (129,807 total units; 118,428 rent-assisted units)

Source: Property and unit counts are based on CRS analysis of HUD data, including the Multifamily Assistance and Section 8 Contracts Database, the Insured Multifamily Mortgages Database, and the 202 Direct Loans database, as of September 30, 2009. [a] Not all units in properties with rental-assistance contracts are covered by those contracts. Where relevant, counts of both rent-assisted units and unassisted units are provided. [b] Rental assistance includes Section 8 (including PAC) as well as RAP and Rent Supplement. It does not include Project Rental Assistance Contracts (PRAC), which are provided to modern Section 202 and Section 811 properties. [c] The term "Rental Assistance Only" means that the property does not have an active Section 236 or Section 221(d)(3)BMIR insured loan or 202 direct loan. However, many of these properties do have other forms of FHA-insured financing or state-aided financing.

APPENDIX B. GLOSSARY

Term	Explanation
Area Median Income	The income levels used by HUD to establish household eligibility for most assisted housing programs. Area median incomes are established by HUD each year for each metropolitan area, parts of some metropolitan areas, and each non-metropolitan county, and they are adjusted for family size.
Affordability Restriction	An agreement between HUD and a property owner that limits the amount of rent a property owner can charge to residents of the property in exchange for HUD financing and/or rental assistance. The restriction may last for the length of the assistance contract or some longer or shorter period.
ELIHPA	Acronym for the Emergency Low-Income Housing Preservation Act, a law that prevented owners of Section 221(d)(3) BMIR and Section 236 properties from prepaying their mortgages unless certain conditions were met. ELIHPA was enacted in 1987 and was replaced by LIHPRHA in 1990.
Fair Market Rent (FMR)	FMRs are established by HUD and are meant to represent the gross rent level needed to obtain modest housing in a community. They are used as a part of the Section 8 contract renewal process, in some circumstances. FMRs are determined for metropolitan areas, non-metropolitan counties, and states. For most areas, the FMR is set at the 40th percentile rent paid by recent movers, which means that the rents for 40% of all standard quality rental housing units rented within the past 18 months are at or below the FMR. For some high cost areas, the FMR is set at the 50th percentile rent or the median rent, so that the rents for 50% of standard units are at or below the FMR.
FHA Mortgage Insurance	Insurance provided by HUD's Federal Housing Administration to protect private lenders in case of borrower default. FHA insures loans for both single-family and multifamily properties.

Flexible Subsidy Program	A program that provided loans to properties with HUD-assisted financing having financial difficulties. Congress gave HUD the authority to provide flexible subsidy assistance in 1978, and FY1995 was the last year in which Congress provided new obligation authority for the program.
Housing Preservation Program	A form of a Section 8 project-based contract that was provided as an incentive for owners with HUD-assisted financing to keep their properties affordable. Congress gave HUD the authority to enter into these contracts in 1987, and the program was terminated in 1998.
LIHPRHA	Acronym for Low-Income Housing Preservation and Resident Homeownership Act, a law that replaced ELIHPA as a means to prevent private owners from prepaying Section 221(d)(3) BMIR and Section 236 mortgages except under certain circumstances. LIHPRHA was enacted in 1990, and Congress stopped providing funding to HUD for preservation incentives to owners in FY1998.
LMSA	Acronym for Loan Management Set Aside, a form of Section 8 rental assistance provided to properties with HUD-assisted financing that were financially troubled, including those financed through the Section 202 loan program, the Section 221(d)(3) BMIR program, and the Section 236 program. HUD provided assistance from 1976 through 1994.
Low-Income Households	Term used by HUD to describe households with income at or below 80% of the area median income.
MAHRA	Acronym for Multifamily Assisted Housing Reform and Accountability Act. Enacted in 1996, the law established procedures and authority for the renewal of expiring Section 8 contracts, including the Mark-to-Market process.
RAP	Acronym for Rental Assistance Payment program, an early form of rental-assistance contract attached to properties with HUD-assisted financing. RAP replaced the Rent Supplement program in 1974. Most RAP units were converted to Section 8 assistance in 1980s.

Rent Supplement	The first form of rental-assistance contract, it was attached to properties with HUD-assisted financing. Most Rent Supplement units were converted to Section 8 assistance in the early 1980s.
Section 202 Loan Program	A HUD program providing direct, low-interest loans to nonprofit developers for the construction of affordable housing for persons who are elderly or have a disability. The program was created in 1959 and extended loans until the early 1990s. In 1990, the loan program was replaced with the Section 202 capital grant program.
Section 202 Capital Grant Program	The current version of the Section 202 program. In 1990, Congress changed the financing mechanism in the Section 202 program from direct loans to capital grants. The capital grants need not be repaid as long as the owner provides housing that is affordable to very low-income elderly residents for at least 40 years.
Section 221(d)(3) BMIR Program	A HUD FHA mortgage insurance program that insured and subsidized below-market interest rate (BMIR) loans for affordable housing developments. The program was active from 1961 to 1968.
Section 236 Program	A HUD FHA mortgage insurance program that provided below-market financing through Interest Reduction Payments for affordable housing developments, active from 1968 to 1973.
Section 8 Project-Based Rental Assistance	Program created in 1974 to provide rental-assistance contracts to newly constructed and substantially rehabilitated properties. The program was later expanded to provide contracts to certain existing properties with HUD-assisted financing (see LMSA). The authority to provide contracts for new units was repealed in 1983.
Section 8 Property Disposition	Form of Section 8 contract provided to properties that defaulted on HUD-assisted financing and were sold by HUD to new owners.
Very Low-Income Households	Term used by HUD to describe households with income at or below 50% of the area median income

End Notes

[1] For more information about federally assisted housing, see CRS Report RL34591, *Overview of Federal Housing Assistance Programs and Policy*, by Maggie McCarty et al.

[2] In some cases, not all units in properties with rental assistance contracts receive rental assistance. For example, it is possible that in a 100 unit building, only 80 units may receive rental assistance. *Figure 1* does not include unassisted units in properties that have rental assistance contracts for some units but that do not receive financing assistance (i.e. no BMIR/236/202). As shown in *Appendix A*, there are a total of 1,136,783 units in properties with rental assistance contracts without financing assistance.

[3] Mortgage insurance encourages private lenders to make loans they would not otherwise offer, or make loans at rates lower than they would otherwise offer, because the insurance protects the lender from financial losses resulting from default.

[4] The Section 202 program is codified at 12 U.S.C. § 1701q. Regulations can be found at 24 C.F.R. §§ 891.100 -891.865. Relevant HUD Handbooks are 4350.3, "Occupancy Requirements for Subsidized Multifamily Housing Programs," and 4571.3, "Section 202 Supportive Housing for the Elderly." For more information, see CRS Report RL33508, *Section 202 and Other HUD Rental Housing Programs for Low-Income Elderly Residents*, by Libby Perl.

[5] See the Cranston-Gonzalez National Affordable Housing Act (P.L. 101-625). These newer units also receive rental assistance, referred to as PRAC (Project Rental-assistance Contracts). PRAC is also used as a rental subsidy in the Section 811 Housing for Persons with Disabilities program.

[6] Barbara A. Haley and Robert W. Gray, *Section 202 Supportive Housing for the Elderly: Program Status and Performance Measure*, U.S. Department of Housing and Urban Development, Office of Policy Development and Research, June 2008, p. 20, http://www.huduser.org/Publications/pdf/ sec_202_1.pdf.

[7] The estimated number of Section 202 units is based on CRS analysis of HUD's 202 Direct Loans database as of September 30, 2009.

[8] The Section 221(d)(3) program is codified at 12 U.S.C. § 1715l(d)(3). Regulations can be found at 24 C.F.R. §§ 221.1 - 221.800. The applicable HUD Handbook is 4560.01, "Mortgage Insurance for Multifamily Moderate Income Housing Projects."

[9] Senate Committee on Banking and Currency, *Housing Act of 1961*, Senate report to accompany S. 1922, 87th Cong., 1st sess., S.Rept. 281, May 19, 1961. The Section 221(d)(3) program also contained a market interest rate component, but unlike the BMIR program, it was not designed to ensure affordability. John R. Gallagher, *Nonprofit Housing Rent Supplement ProgramUnder Section 221(d)(3) of the National Housing Act* (Washington, DC: Urban America, Inc., 1968), p. 4.

[10] Leonard Garland Gaston, "The 221(d)(3) Below Market Interest Rate and Rent Supplement Housing Program" (Ph.D. dissertation, Ohio State University, 1969), p. 120.

[11] John R. Gallagher and John J. O'Donnell, *Nonprofit Housing Under Section 221(d)(3) of the National Housing Act* (Washington, DC: Urban America, Inc., 1966), p. 20.

[12] HUD Handbook 4350.3, chapter 3, paragraph 3-6. For 2009 BMIR rents, see http://www.huduser.org/datasets/il/il09/ IncomeLimits_236_ BHMIR. pdf.

[13] Ibid., chapter 5, paragraph 5-29.

[14] U.S. Department of Housing and Urban Development, *FY2011 Congressional Budget Justifications*, p. L-1, http://hud.gov/offices/cfo/ reports/2011/cjs/Rental_Housing_ Assistance_Program_2010.pdf (hereinafter, *FY2011 HUD Budget Justifications*).

[15] The Section 221(d)(3) program also included a Market Rate program that did not feature mortgage subsidies. However, some Section 221(d)(3) Market Rate properties received additional assistance in the form of Rent Supplement contracts, conditioned on use restrictions similar to those in the BMIR program. The Section 221(d)(3) Market Rate program created roughly 80,000 units in 1,034 properties subject to use restrictions. *Preventing the Disappearance of Low-Income Housing,* Hearing before the Subcommittee on Housing and Community Development of the Committee on Banking, Finance, and Urban Affairs, House of Representatives, 100th Cong., 2nd Sess., June 8, 1988, p. 61.

[16] The estimate of BMIR units is based on CRS analysis of the HUD Mortgages Currently Insured database, as of September 30, 2009.

[17] The Section 236 program is codified at 12 U.S.C. § 1715z-1. Regulations can be found at 24 C.F.R. §§ 236.1-236.1001. The applicable HUD Handbook is 4350.3, "Occupancy Requirements of Subsidized Multifamily Housing Programs."

[18] Congress appropriated funds for new Section 236 developments until 1973, when the Nixon Administration determined that it would make no new funding commitments to federally subsidized housing programs. Although this moratorium on new subsidized housing ended in 1974 with the enactment of that year's Housing and Community Development Act (P.L. 93-383), the Section 236 program was not revived.

[19] 12 U.S.C. §1715z-1(j).

[20] 12 U.S.C. §1715z-1(a).

[21] 12 U.S.C. §1715z-1(c).

[22] HUD was also authorized to make IRP payments to some owners of properties that did not have FHA mortgage insurance. Specifically, the statute permitted HUD to make IRP payments to properties "whose mortgages were made by State or local housing finance agencies or State or local government agencies." 12 U.S.C. § 1715z-1(r). These properties are referred to as state-aided properties.

[23] Hearing before the Senate Special Committee on Aging, Subcommittee on Housing for the Elderly, *Adequacy of Federal Response to Housing Needs of Older Americans*, 92nd Cong., 1st sess., August 2, 1971, p. 130.

[24] House Committee on Banking, Finance and Urban Affairs, Subcommittee on Housing and Community Development, *Preventing the Disappearance of Low Income Housing*, 100th Cong., 2nd sess., June 8, 1988, p. 4.

[25] HUD Handbook 4350.3, chapter 3, paragraphs 3-6 and 3-8. Recent income limits are available at http://www.huduser.org/portal/datasets/il.html.

[26] 12 U.S.C. § 1715z-1(f).

[27] Ibid. Note that HUD has the authority to set higher, market-based, basic and market rents for units with rentalassistance.

[28] *FY2011 HUD Budget Justifications*, p. M-2.

[29] *Preventing the Disappearance of Low-Income Housing,* Hearing before the Subcommittee on Housing and Community Development of the Committee on Banking, Finance, and Urban Affairs, House of Representatives, 100th Congress, 2nd Session, June 8, 1988.

[30] Figure based on CRS analysis of data from the Insured Multifamily Mortgages Database.

[31] *FY2011 HUD Budget Justifications*, p. M-1.

[32] The Rent Supplement program is codified at 12 U.S.C. § 1701s. Regulations can be found at 24 CFR § 215, as in effect immediately before May 1, 1995. The applicable HUD Handbook is 4350.3, "Occupancy Requirements of Subsidized Multifamily Housing Programs."

[33] The program was initially developed to supplement Section 221(d)(3) units; however, when the Section 221(d)(3) program was replaced with the Section 236 program in 1968 (P.L. 90-448), Section 236 units were made eligible for Rent Supplement contracts in the same law.

[34] 12 U.S.C. § 1701s(d) and 12 U.S.C. § 1715z-1(f).

[35] 12 U.S.C. § 1701s(j)(1)(d).

[36] *FY2011 HUD Budget Justifications*, p. L-1.

[37] See Department of Housing and Urban Development FY2010 Budget Justifications, p. N-1, http://www.hud.gov/offices/cfo/reports /2010/cjs/ hsg2010.pdf. On May 19, 1992, a Notice of Funding Availability (NOFA) entitled "Fund Availability (NOFA) for the Conversion of Rent Supplement and Rental-assistance Program Units to Section 8 Assistance" was published at 57 *Federal Register* 21334 announcing funds for the conversion of Rent Supplement project units to Section 8 assistance under the loan management set-aside program. This conversion was authorized by Title II of the FY1992 Departments of Veterans Affairs and Housing and Urban Development, and Independent Agencies Appropriations Act. About 10 years earlier, a similar conversion from Rent Supplement to Section 8 assistance occurred.

[38] Data taken from archived CRS Report 89-100E, *Trends in Funding and Numbers of Households in HUD-Assisted Housing, Fiscal Years 1975-1989*, by Grace Milgrim, March 9, 1989.

[39] *FY2011 HUD Budget Justifications*, p. L-1.

[40] Data based on CRS analysis of HUD data from the Multifamily Assistance and Section 8 Contracts Database, as of September 30, 2009.

[41] The Rental Assistance Payment program is codified at 12 U.S.C. § 1715z-1(f)(2). Regulations can be found at 24 CFR §§ 236.701-765. The applicable HUD Handbook is 4350.3, "Occupancy Requirements of Subsidized Multifamily Housing Programs."

[42] Section 236f(2), as added by Section 212 of the Housing and Community Development Act of 1974.

[43] 24 C.F.R. §236.725.

[44] Data based on CRS analysis of HUD data from the Multifamily Assistance and Section 8 Contracts Database, as of September 30, 2009.

[45] The Section 8 program is codified at 42 U.S.C. § 1437f. Regulations can be found at 24 CFR §§ 880-888. The applicable HUD Handbook is 4350.3, "Occupancy Requirements of Subsidized Multifamily Housing Programs."

[46] The authorizing statute permitted contract terms of up to 20 years for most properties and up to 40 years for stateaided properties. See U.S. Housing Act of 1937, Section 8(e)(1), as added by the Housing and Community Development Act of 1974.

[47] See 42 U.S.C. § 1437f(c), 1976 edition.

[48] See 42 U.S.C. § 1437f(c)(5)-(7), 1976 edition, and 42 U.S.C. § 1437n(c), 2009 edition.

[49] The authorizing statute specified that contracts could be no less than one month and no more than 15 months. See 42 U.S.C. § 1437f(d), 1976 edition. 50 42 USC §1437f(c).

[51] Following criticism of the program for high expense and mismanagement, authority for Section 8 Moderate Rehabilitation contracts was repealed in 1991. Section 289(b) of P.L. 101-625 repealed authority for the Mod Rehab program, effective October 1, 1991, except with respect to single room occupancy dwellings for homeless individuals. For more information on problems with the Moderate Rehabilitation program, see U.S. Congress, Senate Committee on Banking, Housing, and Urban Affairs, Subcommittee on HUD/Mod Rehab Investigation, *Final Report and Recommendations*, Committee Print, 101st Cong., 2 sess., S. Prt. 101-124 (Washington: GPO, 1990).

[52] While the authority for Section 8 contracts on new properties was repealed, HUD continued to provide Section 8 project-based rental-assistance contracts through programs such as LMSA and Property Disposition for several years after the repeal.

[53] The original voucher program was created as a five-year demonstration. It was reauthorized and made permanent by the Housing and Community Development Act of 1987 (P.L. 100-242).

[54] The current Section 8 voucher program is similar to the previous Section 8 existing program, in that it provides portable rent subsidies for families to use in the housing of their choice. It was initially created in the early 1980s and it fully replaced the Section 8 existing program in 1998. For more information, see CRS Report RL32284, *An Overview of the Section 8 Housing Programs*, by Maggie McCarty.

[55] The regulations governing LMSA can be found at 24 C.F.R. § 886 Part A and the relevant HUD Handbook is HUD Handbook 4350.2, "Section 8 Loan Management Set-Aside Program for Projects."

[56] The interim rule establishing the program was published in 41 *Federal Register* 12170, March 23, 1976.

[57] For Section 221(d)(3) BMIR, Section 236, and Section 202, Section 8 subsidies were the difference between the previously established rent for the unit and the tenant contribution (24 C.F.R. § 886.118).

[58] 24 C.F.R. § 886.112. Contract rents are generally adjusted annually based on the AAF. The AAF is derived from data on residential housing costs in particular market areas. In some cases, HUD can also make rent adjustments based on property-specific budget needs, at the request of the owner.

[59] U.S. General Accounting Office, *Section 8 Project-Based Rental Assistance: HUD's Processes for Evaluating and Using Unexpended Balances Are Ineffective*, GAO/RCED-98-202, July 1998, p. 14, http://www.gao. gov/ archive/1998/rc98202.pdf.

[60] See § 181 of P.L. 100-242.

[61] The regulations governing Property Disposition can be found at 24 C.F.R. § 886 Part C.

[62] U.S. General Accounting Office, *Section 8 Project-Based Rental Assistance: HUD's Processes for Evaluating and Using Unexpended Balances are Ineffective*, GAO/RCED-98-202, July 1998, p. 16, http://www. gao. Gov /archive/1998/rc98202.pdf.

[63] Ibid. p. 16.

[64] Data based on CRS analysis of HUD data from the Multifamily Assistance and Section 8 Contracts Database, as of September 30, 2009.

[65] 24 C.F.R. §§ 888.111 through 888.420.

[66] PBCAs are all PHAs, and most are also State Housing Finance Agencies. They are paid a fee by HUD to manage the contracts, including ensuring that HAPs are paid, conducting management and occupancy reviews, and following up after physical inspections.

[67] The ability of HUD to renew contracts is subject to appropriations from Congress. Generally, Congress has provided sufficient appropriations for HUD to renew all contracts with owners who wish to renew.

[68] Sara E. Johnson, "In Depth Review of the Title VI Program," Prepared for the Making LIHPRHA Work Conference, Washington, DC, October 8, 1992, p. A-19 (hereinafter, "In Depth Review of the Title VI Program"). The rights of forprofit (limited dividend) owners to prepay were outlined in regulation. For Section 236, see 24 C.F.R. § 236.30 (1971) and for Section 221(d)(3), see 24 C.F.R. § 221.524 (1969).

[69] The National Low Income Housing Preservation Commission, *Preventing the Disappearance of Low-Income Housing*, Report to Congress, Washington, DC, 1988, p. 19 (hereinafter, *Preventing the Disappearance of Low-Income Housing*).

[70] U.S. Department of Housing and Urban Development, Notice PIH 01-41, *Section 8 Tenant-Based Assistance (Enhanced and Regular Housing Choice Vouchers) for Housing Conversion Actions: Policy and Processing Guidance*, issued November 14, 2001, pp. 21-22 (hereinafter, HUD Notice PIH 01-41).

[71] 24 C.F.R. § 236.30(a)(1)(i) (1995) and 24 C.F.R. § 221.524(a)(1)(ii) (1995).

[72] HUD Notice PIH 01-41, pp. 18-24.

[73] Meryl Finkel et al., *Multifamily Properties: Opting In, Opting Out and Remaining Affordable*, Department of Housing and Urban Development, Prepared by Econometrica and Abt Associates, Washington, DC, January 2006, p.14, http://www.huduser.org/Publications/pdf/opting_in.pdf (hereinafter, *Multifamily Properties: Opting In, Opting Out and Remaining Affordable*).

[74] HUD Notice PIH 01-41, p. 19.

[75] P.L. 106-569 further gave Section 202 owners the ability to refinance their mortgages if they obtain a loan with a lower interest rate, and if the new loan results in reduced debt service (i.e. reduced principal and interest payments). These requirements have made it difficult (if not impossible) for owners of older Section 202 developments—those with interest rates at about 3%—to refinance due to an inability to find lower interest rates.

[76] U.S. Department of Housing and Urban Development, Notice H 02-16, *Prepayment of Direct Loans on Section 202 and 202/8 Projects with Inclusion of FHA Mortgage Insurance Guidelines*, issued August 23, 2002, p. 3 (hereinafter, HUD Notice H 02-16).

[77] In addition, if owners applied to HUD for permission to prepay and followed HUD prepayment requirements, they would be exempt from the requirements of the Multifamily Assisted Housing Reform and Accountability Act (MAHRA). Provisions exempting Section 202 owners who refinance pursuant to P.L. 106-569 were codified as part of the FY2002 Departments of Labor, and Health and Human Services, and Education Appropriations Act (P.L. 107-116). See Section 612(h). For more information, see the "Section 8 Expiring Contracts, Renewals, and the Multifamily Assisted Housing Reform and Accountability Act (MAHRA)" section of this report.

[78] HUD Notice H 02-16, pp. 11-12. However, if the owner was also opting out of a Section 8 contract, then tenants receiving Rent Supplement assistance would receive enhanced vouchers. HUD Notice PIH 01-41, p. 18.

[79] Ibid., pp. 9-10.

[80] If the property also had assisted financing, it is possible that the property could continue to be subject to affordability restrictions after the expiration of the rental-assistance contract.

[81] This is assuming the jurisdiction in which the property is located has not adopted local rent control or rent stabilization policies.

[82] *Multifamily Properties: Opting In, Opting Out and Remaining Affordable*, p. 15.

[83] Tenants can receive enhanced vouchers if the property includes a project-based Section 8 contract that is also expiring. For more information, see HUD Notice PIH 01-41.

[84] The standards can be found at 24 C.F.R. Part 200, Subpart S, §§ 200.925 through 200.955.

[85] HUD has adopted a "3-2-1" model, where properties that have the highest inspection scores are only inspected every three years, properties with good scores are inspected every two years, and properties with troubled scores are inspected every year.

[86] The scoring process is described in 24 C.F.R. Part 200, Subpart P, §§ 200.850 through 200.857.

[87] Regardless of the score, any exigent health and safety concerns must be mitigated immediately and written notification must be provided to HUD within three days. 24 C.F.R. § 200.857(c)(2).

[88] While the regulation (24 C.F.R. § 200.857(h)) requires that any property with a score below 30 be automatically referred to the DEC, HUD changed its procedures as of November 1, 2002, so that any property with a score below 60 is now referred to the DEC. See January 16, 2003, Memorandum from Beverly J. Miller, Director, Office of Multifamily Asset Management, subject: Properties With Inspection Scores Under 60 Points, http://www.hud.gov/offices/hsg/mfh/hto/60points.pdf.

[89] See 24 CFR § 200.857(i).

[90] U.S. Department of Housing and Urban Development, *FY2009 Performance and Accountability Report*, November 16, 2009, p. 135, http://hud.gov /offices/cfo/reports /hudfy2009par.pdf (hereinafter *FY2009 Performance and Accountability Report*).

[91] The average number of exigent health and safety violations found in failing properties was 2.73, which is a significant decrease from the average of 7.6 in FY2006. *FY2009 Performance and Accountability Report*, p. 118.

[92] 24 C.F.R. Part 5 Subpart H, §§ 200.210 through 200.245.

[93] Department of Housing and Urban Development, "Industry User Guide for the Financial Assessment Subsystem—Multifamily Housing (FASSUB)," Release 7.0.0.0, http://www.disasterhousing.gov/offices/reac/products/fass/fassmf_pdfs/chap1_introduction.pdf.

[94] *FY2009 Performance and Accountability Report*, p. 136.

[95] *Multifamily Properties: Opting In, Opting Out and Remaining Affordable*, p. 15.

[96] These vouchers are not automatically provided; Congress must first appropriate funding for these vouchers. Congress has typically provided sufficient funding to provide tenant protection and enhanced vouchers to all eligible families.

[97] See HUD Notice PIH 2001-41 for more details about enhanced and tenant protection vouchers.

[98] Specifically, this involves situations where a nonprofit owner sold the property to a for-profit owner but the for-profit owner did not assume the mortgage.

[99] Such as Flexible Subsidy loans, discussed later in this report.

[100] See *Preventing the Disappearance of Low-Income Housing*, footnote 69.

[101] ELIHPA was initially codified at 12 U.S.C. § 1715l, note. Although the text remains, when ELIHPA was superseded by the Low Income Housing Preservation and Resident Homeownership Act (LIHPRHA, P.L. 101-625), the law was moved to 12 U.S.C. §§ 4101 et. seq. ELIHPA was subsequently amended by Title X, Subtitle B of the Stewart B. McKinney Homeless Assistance Act Amendments of 1988 (P.L. 100-628).

[102] P.L. 100-242, Section 233.

[103] See discussion of Housing Preservation Program Section 8 contracts under "Additional Uses of Section 8 Project-Based Rental Assistance" earlier in this report.

[104] Section 224 of P.L. 100-242, as amended by section 1023 of the Stewart B. McKinney Homeless Assistance Act Amendments of 1988 (P.L. 100-628), codified at 12 U.S.C. § 1715l note.

[105] See section 203 of P.L. 100-242 for repeal provisions.

[106] The program was extended three times, through November 30, 1990, so that it would not lapse before the enactment of LIHPRHA. See P.L. 101-235, P.L. 101-402, and P.L. 101-494.

[107] U.S. Congress, Conference Committee, *Housing and Community Development Act of 1987*, report to accompany S. 825, 100th Cong., 1st sess., November 6, 1987, H.Rept. 100-426.

[108] "In Depth Review of the Title VI Program," pp. A-20 to A-21. LIHPRHA was subsequently amended by Title III of the Housing and Community Development Act of 1992 (P.L. 102-550). Congress considered HUD's implementation of P.L. 101-625 "severely deficient in several respects" and provided further direction in the amendments. See U.S. Congress, Senate Committee on Banking, Housing, and Urban Affairs, *The National Affordable Housing Act Amendments of 1992*, report to accompany S. 3031, 102nd Cong., 1st sess., November 23, 1992, S.Rept. 102-332. The provisions in S. 3031 regarding affordable housing preservation were incorporated into P.L. 102-550. LIHPRHA is codified at 12 U.S.C. § 4101 et. seq.

[109] 12 U.S.C. § 4108.

[110] 12 U.S.C. § 4113.

[111] "In Depth Review of the Title VI Program," pp. A-25 to A-26.

[112] Ibid.

[113] 24 C.F.R. § 248.157 and § 248.161 (1993).

[114] 12 U.S.C. § 4114.

[115] In testimony before the Senate Banking Committee's Subcommittee on Housing Opportunity and Community Development, GAO noted that "HUD, HUD's OIG, the House and Senate Committees on Appropriations, and the National Alliance of HUD Tenants have all expressed concerns about the program's high cost—over $1.2 billion or an average of $19,152 per unit for projects that have completed the preservation process." See U.S. General Accounting Office, *Multifamily Housing: Issues and Options to Consider in Revising HUD's Low Income Housing Preservation Program*, T-RCED-96-29, October 17, 1995, p. 2, http://archive.gao.gov/papr2pdf/155409.pdf (hereinafter, *Multifamily Housing: Issues and Options to Consider in Revising HUD's Low Income Housing Preservation Program*).

[116] U.S. General Accounting Office, *Housing Preservation: Policies and Administrative Problems Increase Costs and Hinder Program Operations*, RCED-97-169, July 18, 1997, p. 6, http://www.gao.gov/archive /1997/ rc97169.pdf (hereinafter, *Housing Preservation: Policies and Administrative Problems Increase Costs and Hinder Program Operations*).

[117] *Multifamily Housing: Issues and Options to Consider in Revising HUD's Low Income Housing Preservation Program*, p. 7.

[118] *Housing Preservation: Policies and Administrative Problems Increase Costs and Hinder Program Operations*, p. 7.

[119] U.S. Department of Housing and Urban Development, *FY2008 Performance and Accountability Report*, p. 336, http://www.hud.gov/ offices/cfo/reports/hudpar-fy2008.pdf.

[120] See, for example, *Cienega Gardens v. U.S.*, 503 F.3rd 1266 (Fed. Cir. 2007). The plaintiffs in *Cienega Gardens* began their lawsuit in 1994. The Court of Appeals for the Federal Circuit held in 2003 that ELIHPA and LIHPRHA did result in a compensable taking as it applied to four model plaintiffs. However, that court remanded to a lower court for additional proceedings with respect to the claims raised by the other, non-model plaintiffs in the case because the record did not account for the facts of those individual plaintiffs. The lower court subsequently held that ELIHPA and LIHPRHA constituted a compensable taking with regard to the non-model plaintiffs. However, the Court of Appeals for the Federal Circuit, in its latest *Cienega Gardens* decision, vacated the lower court's holding in favor of the nonmodel plaintiffs and remanded for further proceedings to address issues with the lower court's legal analysis. (*Cienega X*, 503 F.3d at 1270.)

[121] See P.L. 104-134, in which Congress stated that "an owner of eligible low-income housing may prepay the mortgage or request voluntary termination of a mortgage insurance contract, so long as the owner agrees not to raise rents for sixty days after prepayment."

[122] The House Appropriations Committee Report accompanying the FY1998 appropriations bill (H.Rept. 105-175) stated that the Committee was not recommending funding for preservation due to the results of a General Accounting Office report showing the high cost of the program. The FY1998 Appropriations Act did provide $10 million "to compensate organizations that incurred costs of appraisals and preparing plans of action." (See Conference Report, H.Rept. 105-297).

[123] 12 U.S.C. § 1715z-1(e)(2).

[124] See U.S. Department of Housing and Urban Development, Notice H 00-08, *Guidelines for Continuation of Interest Reduction Payments after Refinancing*, issued May 16, 2000, pp. 3-4.

[125] The fund was established by P.L. 100-242 § 186(b)(1). Description taken from HUD Handbook 4355.1, "Flexible Subsidy."

[126] P.L. 100-242 § 185(g).

[127] HUD Handbook 4355.1, Chapter 1.

[128] HUD Handbook 4355.1, p. 1-2.

[129] U.S. Department of Housing and Urban Development, *FY2004 Congressional Budget Justifications*, p. H-1, http://hud.gov/offices /cfo/ reports/04estimates/flexible.pdf.

[130] For more information, see U.S. Congress, House Committee on Banking and Financial Services, Subcommittee on Housing and Community Opportunity, *Resolving the FHA Multifamily Portfolio: HUD's Mark-to-Market Proposal*, 104th Cong., 1st sess., June 13, 1995, H.Hrg. 104-21 (Washington, DC: GPO, 1996).

[131] Taken from CRS Report RL31182, *Assisted Housing: Section 8 Mark-to-Market Restructuring*, by Susan M. Vanhorenbeck.

[132] MAHRA is codified at 42 U.S.C. § 1437f note. As a result, this report references the sections of the act rather than the statute.

[133] Department of Housing and Urban Development, *Section 8 Renewal Policy Guidebook*, April 17, 2009, Edition, http://www.hud.gov/offices /hsg/mfh/exp/guide/s8renew.pdf.

[134] Some properties are unable to complete the debt restructuring component of Mark-to-Market, for a variety of reasons, but they still have their rents reduced to market. These properties may be at risk of default, and they are considered "Watch List" properties. They receive a special form of renewal contract, with acknowledgement that they remain eligible and may pursue restructuring at a later date. For more information, see HUD Memorandum, "Revised Guidance on Monitoring OMHAR Watch List Properties," September 27, 2001.

[135] In a payment of claim, HUD makes a payment from the FHA insurance fund to reduce or eliminate the principal balance on an FHA-insured loan.

[136] Generally, the original FHA-insured first mortgage is paid off and replaced with a new, smaller, and often FHAinsured mortgage. The claim paid from the insurance fund is not necessarily forgiven; instead, it can serve as a secondary debt upon which payment is only due if funds are available or at sale or refinancing.

[137] Mark-to-Market Pipeline Summary Report, as of January 21, 2010, available at http://www.hud.gov/offices/hsg/omhar/readingrm/reports.cfm.

[138] The market comparable rent is capped at 150% of local Fair Market Rent, although owners can appeal for a higher rent if their properties serve vulnerable populations, are located in a low-vacancy area, or have strong community support.

[139] HUD does have the authority to approve discretionary Mark-up-to-Markets for properties that would otherwise be ineligible, if they meet certain criteria, including properties that serve a vulnerable population, are located in an area with low vacancy rates, or have strong community support.

[140] Another subset of properties participated in HUD's earlier Portfolio Reengineering Demonstration program (under LIPHRA and ELIHPA). Those properties, in some cases, are required to renew their contracts, and, in other cases, can choose to renew under any option for which they qualify.

[141] Some owners do not have the option to opt-out; for example, owners who participated in earlier preservation initiatives and must maintain affordability for a certain period of time.

[142] See the FY2009 HUD appropriations law (P.L. 111-8, Section 218 and Section 212) and the FY2010 HUD appropriations law (P.L. 111-117, Sections 217 and 212).

[143] HUD Press Release No. 10-057, "HUD Program Brings Seniors Back Home to New Orleans: Grants will transform and upgrade public housing programs while creating jobs," March 26, 2010.

[144] See HUD Notice H 09-02, *Green Retrofit Program for Multifamily Housing (GRP)*, May 13, 2009.

[145] See, for example, U.S. General Accounting Office, *More Accessible HUD Data Could Help Efforts to Preserve Housing for Low-Income Tenants*, GAO-04-20, January 2004, pp. 4-5, http://www.gao.gov/new.items/ d0420.pdf.

[146] See, for example, *Multifamily Properties: Opting In, Opting Out and Remaining Affordable*, p vii. This HUD study examined the characteristics of properties where owners prepaid their mortgages or opted out of rental-assistance contracts (or both) and compared them to properties that remained in the affordable housing stock. Among the findings were that owners in neighborhoods with higher market rents as well as those with older properties left the stock at higher rates.

[147] For example, see Mark Shroder and Arthur Reiger, "Vouchers versus Production Revisited," Journal of Housing Research, vol. 11, no. 1, which finds that the Section 8 certificate (voucher) program is less expensive than the original Section 8 program.

[148] Edgar O. Olsen, *Achieving Fundamental Housing Policy Reform*, Department of Economics, University of Virginia, April 24, 2006.

[149] For example, while the Millennial Housing Commission's Final Report recommended expanding the voucher program, it also recommended preserving the existing stock of assisted housing as well as using new production resources. For a discussion of the role of project-based assistance, see Jill Khadduri and Charles Wilkins, "Designing Subsidized Housing Programs: What Have We Learned?," in *Revisiting Rental Housing: Policies, Programs, and Priorities*, ed. Nicolas P. Retsinas and Eric S. Belsky (Washington, DC: Brookings Institution, 2008), pp. 163-164.

[150] The Section 202 Supportive Housing for the Elderly program, the Section 811 Supportive Housing for Persons with Disabilities program, and the HOPE VI program each provides capital funds for new construction of assisted housing. However the HOPE VI program does not create new units; it replaces existing units.

[151] See, for example, The MacArthur Foundation, *Window of Opportunity: Preserving Affordable Rental Housing*, http://www.macfound.org /site/c. lkLXJ8MQKrH/b.4278471 /apps/s /contentasp?ct=4620007. The Mac Arthur Foundation reported spending half the cost of a new rental housing unit to preserve 45,000 units of existing rental housing.

[152] For example, see Sandra J. Newman Ann B. Schnare, "And A Suitable Living Environment for All: The Failure of Housing Programs to Deliver on Housing Quality," *Housing Policy*

Debate, vol. 8 issue 4, 1997, http://www.mi.vt.edu/data/files /hpd%208(4)/hpd%208(4)_ newman.pdf, which found that the federally assisted housing stock was more concentrated in "underclass" areas than the private market stock of housing or where families with vouchers had chosen to live. However, it was less concentrated than public housing.

[153] See, for example, Leonard F. Heumann, Karen Winter-Nelson, and James R. Anderson, *The 1999 National Survey of Section 202 Elderly Housing*, American Association of Retired Persons, January 2001, p. 7, http://assets.aarp.org/rgcenter/il/2001_02_housing.pdf.

[154] The Center for Housing Policy/National Housing Institute has a useful explanation of recapitalization in the context of housing preservation: "Many multifamily developments need to be recapitalized after a certain number of years to cover the costs of deferred maintenance and upgrades to bring them into conformity with current living standards. Affordable multifamily homes also need to be recapitalized periodically, but because of legal or practical limitations on permissible rents, it is difficult to support new debt for this purpose." See http://www.housingpolicy. org/glossary.html#R.

[155] Data as of September 30, 2008.

[156] *Multifamily Properties: Opting In, Opting Out and Remaining Affordable*, p. 24.

[157] Ibid., p. 25.

[159] For the purposes of this analysis, properties with Section 8 contracts include properties with Project Assistance Contracts (PAC). PAC contracts were provided from about 1988 to 1990 to properties with Section 202 loans where the properties were designated for persons with disabilities. The PAC was provided in lieu of Section 8 project-based rental-assistance.

[160] Because some rental assistance contracts do not cover all units in a building, there are approximately 117,317 units in properties with rental assistance contracts that are not themselves rent-assisted.

[161] See, for example, the Affordable Housing Preservation Tax Relief Act (H.R. 2887), the Section 202 Supportive Housing for the Elderly Act (S. 118), and the Housing Preservation and Tenant Protection Act (H.R. 4868), all of which were introduced in the 111th Congress.

[162] A group made up of numerous housing organizations released preservation recommendations in 2007. See National Preservation Working Group, *Legislative Provisions to Support the Preservation of Affordable Housing*, April 2007, http://content.knowledgeplex.org/ kp2/ cache/documents /3747/374781.pdf.

[163] 12 U.S.C. § 1715z-1a(d).

[164] See HUD Handbook 4350.1, Chapter 25-11.

[165] The amount of capital gains depends on the basis of the property upon sale. Very simply, the basis is the purchase (or development) price of the property, minus depreciation, plus improvements. Capital gains are the difference between the basis and the sale price.

[166] Under a right of first refusal, an owner must offer a property for purchase to the priority entity, and generally must accept a fair market price if offered by the priority entity before the owner can sell the property to a non-priority entity in the private market. Under a right of first purchase, the priority entity has preference over other private market bidders as long as the offer made by the priority entity is at least equivalent to the other offers made.

[167] Authority has been provided through the annual HUD appropriations acts since FY2006.

[168] U.S. Congress, House Committee on Financial Services, Subcommittee on Housing and Community Opportunity, *Legislative Options for Preserving Federally- and State-Assisted Affordable Housing and Preventing Displacement of Low-Income, Elderly and Disabled Tenants*, 111th Cong., 1st sess., July 15, 2009, H.Hrg. 111-59, http://www.house.gov/apps /list/hearing/financialsvcs_dem/59.pdf. The draft legislation is available at http://www.house.gov/apps/list/ hearing/ financialsvcs_dem/frank_035_xml.pdf.

[169] See the testimony, as printed in U.S. Congress, House Committee on Financial Services, Subcommittee on Housing and Community Opportunity, *Legislative Options for Preserving Federally- and State-Assisted Affordable Housing and Preventing Displacement of Low-Income, Elderly and Disabled Tenants*, Hearing, 111th Cong., 1st sess., July 15, 2009, H. Hrg. 111-59 (Washington: GPO, 2009).

[170] U.S. Congress, House Committee on Financial Services, Subcommittee on Housing and Community Opportunity, *H.R. 4868, Housing Preservation and Tenant Protection Act of 2010*, March 24, 2010.

[171] 12 U.S.C. § 1701q, note.

[172] A similar proposal for refinancing Section 202 loans was included in the FY2009 and FY2010 appropriations acts; however, these changes were only in effect for the duration of the fiscal years covered by the appropriations laws.

[173] However, some pre-1974 properties received rental assistance later through the Rent Supplement program and the Loan Management Set Aside program.

In: HUD-Assisted Housing Preservation
Editors: J. Moran and A. Davies
ISBN: 978-1-61324-856-0

Chapter 2

TESTIMONY OF TAMMYE TREVINO, ADMINISTRATOR, RURAL HOUSING SERVICE, U.S. DEPARTMENT OF AGRICULTURE, BEFORE THE SUBCOMMITTEE ON HOUSING AND COMMUNITY OPPORTUNITY*

July 15, 2009

Chairwoman Waters, Ranking Member Capito, and members of the Committee, thank you for the opportunity to appear before you to discuss multi-family housing preservation in rural America. This is a critically important issue and in broad terms we believe that the strategy outlined in H.R. 2876 and in the discussion draft before the Committee is promising. I would like to thank all those involved with this legislation, both in this session of Congress and in previous session, for your hard work. I am pleased to testify before you today on behalf of Secretary Tom Vilsack, Under Secretary Dallas Tonsager, and USDA Rural Development's Housing Programs, and look forward to working with you and the Committee to further the preservation agenda.

* This is an edited, reformatted and augmented version of a Testimony given by Tammye Trevino, Administrator, Rural Housing Service, U.S. Department of Agriculture, Before the Subcommittee on Housing and Community Opportunity, on July 15, 2009.

At USDA, we advocate a strong national housing policy that both supports the American dream of homeownership and provides affordable rental opportunities. I would also note that as the number of privately-financed foreclosures continues to increase in these difficult economic times, more Americans, especially in rural areas, are relying on rental properties than in years past.We are greatly encouraged by the committee's focus on legislation that will create national housing preservation standards for all government agencies that specialize in housing assistance, especially in rural communities.

For 60 years, our rural housing programs have provided invaluable support for low and very-low income families in rural areas. These programs currently include the Section 502 Single Family Housing Direct and Guaranteed Loan programs, the Section 515 Rural Rental Housing Direct Loan program, and the Section 538 Rural Rental Housing Guaranteed Loan program. I look forward to working closely with Secretary Vilsack, Congress, and the administration to strengthen these, and especially the direct loan programs.

The USDA rural housing portfolio as of May 2009 accounts for over 650,500 direct and guaranteed single- and multi-family loans at a value of more than $53 billion. This includes 332,000 single-family direct loans for $14 billion; 293,000 single-family guaranteed loans for $28 billion; 25,500 multi-family direct loans for $11 billion; and 288 multi-family guaranteed loans for $350 million.

In an era in which private sector foreclosure numbers are higher than they have been in a generation, the Rural Housing Service has experienced low default and foreclosure rates. In 2009, the Rural Housing Service direct loan program has 10,477 foreclosures in process, less than 50 percent of which we estimate will result in actual foreclosures as we work with our homeowners to help them stay in their homes. The foreclosures in process represent approximately 3.4 percent of the agency's 502 direct Single Family portfolio. In May 2009, the Mortgage Bankers Association reported that 3.85% of borrowers nationally were facing foreclosure. In addition to our success in mitigating foreclosures, thus far in Fiscal Year 2009 we have funded over 86,000 loans and on July 1st we hit the $10 billion mark in the Single Family Guaranteed housing program. Moreover, we have funded 8,000 Section 502 Single Family direct loans totaling over $940 million in 2009, almost 20 percent of which were funded through the Recovery Act.

In 2008, our Section 538 Guaranteed Rural Rental Housing Program made loan guarantee commitments to build or repair 118 properties using $132 million in loan guarantees. These commitments have or will generate a total of more than $660 million in construction activity building or repairing 5,457 apartments in rural America. Of this total, more than 40 percent was used to preserve existing section 515 properties. The Section 538 guaranteed multi-family housing program has attracted more than four dollars of investor equity or other funding to these transactions for every one dollar of loan guarantee commitment. The government's direct one-time cost to build or repair these apartments is approximately $2,300 per apartment.

The $11.5 billion direct multi-family housing portfolio financed by USDA Rural Development has over 15,900 Section 515 rural rental housing properties financed primarily by 50-year 1 percent loans and Section 514/516 farm labor housing properties financed by 1 percent loans and grants. The two programs have been providing decent, safe, and sanitary affordable rental housing since the 1960's to countless rural Americans.

Rural Development multi-family housing programs were established because sufficient access to capital and credit was not available to serve the needs of very low-income renters who wished to live and work in rural communities. Although the overall capacity of the American credit system has grown since the middle of the last century, low-income rural residents continue to be underserved. The difficult economic times we are now experiencing add to the stress.

We therefore face two immediate challenges. The first is the ability to provide new affordable rental housing units. The second is the rehabilitation and revitalization of a critically important but now aging rural rental portfolio. We are here today to discuss the latter.

The Committee raised six specific questions, and I would like very briefly to address each of them in turn:

- How will the Housing preservation and Tenant Protection Act improve affordable housing preservation policy at the federal, state and local level?

While we are still studying the proposed legislation and may have questions regarding the implementation of certain aspects of it, the proposed legislation appears to provide the Agency with a number of revitalization tools that would provide cost effective preservation options for the existing multi-family housing rental housing portfolio so that these projects can continue to serve their communities throughout rural America. The proposed legislation contains voucher authority that will help protect tenants in properties that leave the program.

- What are the benefits of preserving existing affordable housing compared with new construction?

The benefits of preserving existing housing are clear; it is less expensive, roughly one-third to one-quarter the cost of new construction; it can be accomplished faster, with site and acquisition issues already resolved; it presents many opportunities to upgrade energy conservation; and it minimizes the NIMBY effect since most communities welcome an upgrade to existing rental properties in place.

- What type of tools or statutory authority are needed for RHS to better assist states, local government and preservation oriented entities in preserving existing affordable housing?
- In general, the tools provided by the proposed bill would help RHS and its partners revitalize the existing portfolio. However, we would like to work with the
- Committee to ensure that the tools will provide the best possible options to support these critical revitalization efforts.
- Please describe any statutory, regulatory (including staffing levels), fiscal, and/or legal barriers limiting or prohibiting preservation transactions.

Currently, our revitalization program is authorized only as a demonstration program, not in permanent authorization legislation. The lack of permanent authorization makes it difficult for the agency to promulgate permanent program regulations and to address long term issues, including the length of vouchers. Further, we need to determine the resources needed to accomplish the goals we establish and we will develop those estimates during the budget formulation process. Specifically we need to examine what types and amounts of resources will be needed to work with a larger portfolio level of transactions, assure quality control, and provide for consistent processing throughout the country.

- Please discuss the impact if any of the foreclosure crisis on RHS assisted multifamily properties and the impact of the foreclosure crisis on RHS assisted properties that have been at risk of foreclosure.
- We have not seen an increase in the foreclosure rate of RHS assisted multi-family properties. We know that there are some individuals who

have lost their homes in the current economic downturn who have applied for housing,

- Please share any other views you may have on the discussion draft.
- Rural Development's Section 514 and 516 programs, providing for financing of farm labor housing, are important components of our housing portfolio. We look forward to working with the Committee in addressing the preservation needs of these rental housing resources as well.

The inclusion of voucher authority in the proposed legislation will help protect tenants in properties that leave the program. At the present time, in a Section 515 property where the mortgage is prepaid either by borrower action or through foreclosure, the property owner can increase rents to market rates. At the same time, by leaving the 515 program, the property is no longer eligible for Rental Assistance. The current Rural Development demonstration voucher program provides protection against rent increases or the tenant having to relocate as a result of prepayment or foreclosure.

Our demonstration voucher program is in its fourth year and has been highly successful. Over the last three years, more than $13.5 million in voucher funds have been obligated and over 3,500 new and renewed vouchers have been provided to rural residents. Over 90% of voucher recipients have elected to remain in the property they have called home for a period of years. The intention behind this "soft landing" voucher approach was to provide a simple, direct and responsive solution to an immediate and growing problem without duplicating other federal rental assistance programs.

We also continue on a demonstration basis to carry out many of the objectives authorized by the proposed bill in regard to a long-term viability plan. In our multi-family housing units, we are conducting physical needs assessments with an emphasis on our older properties. We also offer a range of financial tools that include loan restructuring and rent adjustments. This approach has helped to contain growing foreclosure and default rates in these tough economic times.

The early results of our restructuring demonstration are extremely encouraging. When the initial application window closed on April 17, 2006, approximately 4,000 Section 515 property owners applied for debt restructuring. This represents 25 percent of the total portfolio. In the three full years of implementation as a demonstration program, USDA has obligated over 300 transactions that will improve the housing conditions of 10,000 tenants. These results indicate a tremendous interest among the ownership community in seeking a resolution to the revitalization challenge.

In addition to rural vouchers and debt restructuring, in order for us to successfully carry out our goals, we must also work closely with the other agencies that provide government assisted housing. The proposed legislation makes that goal easier by introducing the concept of a national database that will give us access to the information needed to track America's affordable housing stock.

We realize that the rehabilitation and capital needs of the portfolio are significant. However, at approximately $30,000 per unit, the cost effective rehabilitation tools and our ability to leverage third party financing have actually led to reductions in post-transaction rents, rather than modest increases as first anticipated. The revitalization program has also been designed to provide financing options to both sophisticated developers who work with third party financing and small owners who need affordable, accessible, and relatively simple financing options.

Finally, in cooperation with Secretary Shaun Donovan and the Department of Housing and Urban Development, Secretary Vilsack, Under Secretary Tonsager, and I will ensure that information regarding any covered multi-family properties will be available to the public within the 18-month period after the enactment of this legislation.

Madam Chairwoman, we applaud the efforts of this legislation to include more property owners in this national preservation effort. It is my goal to assist Secretary Vilsack and President Obama in working with the Committee and our public and private partners to spur economic growth and create a lasting foundation in the heart of rural America.

I was born, raised, and lived most of my life in rural south Texas. I have worked and advocated for the development of rural communities for most of my career. I understand the challenges facing rural communities and the struggles that many families in rural America face every day.

Thank you for allowing me to share our Department of Agriculture perspective as you address this important issue. I am available to answer your questions now or at any time in the future.

In: HUD-Assisted Housing Preservation ISBN: 978-1-61324-856-0
Editors: J. Moran and A. Davies

Chapter 3

STATEMENT OF TOBY HALLIDAY VICE PRESIDENT, NATIONAL HOUSING TRUST PRESENTED TO THE SUBCOMMITTEE ON HOUSING AND COMMUNITY OPPORTUNITY HOUSE COMMITTEE ON FINANCIAL SERVICES*

July 15, 2009

Subcommittee Chairwoman Waters, and Ranking Member Capito, Chairman Frank and Ranking Member Bachus, and members of the Committee, thank you for inviting me to testify today. My

name is Toby Halliday, and I am Vice President for Public Policy for the National Housing Trust. Let me also thank Subcommittee Chairwoman Waters and Chairman Frank for convening this hearing and for your leadership on this important issue. I'd also like to thank all the members of this Committee who have supported legislative efforts to preserve and revitalize our nation's limited supply of decent, safe, affordable rental housing.

The National Housing Trust ("the Trust") is a national nonprofit organization formed in 1986, dedicated exclusively to the preservation and improvement of existing affordable housing. Our Board of Directors includes

* This is an edited, reformatted and augmented version of a Statement given by Toby Halliday Vice President, National Housing Trust Presented to the Subcommittee on Housing and Community Opportunity House Committee on Financial Services, on July 15, 2009.

representatives of all major interests in the preservation field, including tenant advocates, owners and managers, state housing agencies, national and regional nonprofit intermediaries, housing scholars and other housing professionals who care deeply about protecting this irreplaceable resource.

The Trust acts based on a fundamental belief: preserving existing affordable rental housing is the essential first step in solving our nation's housing dilemma. Our public policy advocacy is informed by our direct experiences on the ground preserving affordable housing. The Trust's loan fund, National Housing Trust Community Development Fund, provides loans to other nonprofits to finance affordable housing preservation. The NHT/Enterprise Preservation Corporation, an affiliated organization formed as a joint venture with Enterprise Community Partners, redevelops and owns many federally subsidized properties. Over the past decade, the Trust has helped save and improve more than 20,000 apartments in over 40 states. The vast majority of these apartments have HUD subsidized mortgages or project-based rental assistance contracts.

Today I also testify on behalf of the National Preservation Working Group, a coalition of 25 organizations supporting affordable rental housing. For over 18 years the Preservation Working Group has convened on a regular basis to respond to preservation issues, share best practices among nonprofit preservation practitioners, and discuss and pursue improvements in public policy to facilitate the preservation of decent, affordable rental homes. On behalf of the tenants of assisted housing around the country, residents of the neighborhoods in which these properties exist, and mission minded nonprofit developers, owners, and managers of these properties, the members of the Preservation Working Group thank you for your attention to the critical need to protect affordable rental housing serving urban, suburban, rural and elderly households that is at risk of loss or conversion to other uses. Each individual provision in the draft legislation corrects some flaw or gap in our patchwork of housing programs and policies, and together these national housing policy rests. We welcome the opportunity to work with you to make this proposed legislation become law.

The members of the Preservation Working Group are:

National Housing Trust
National Low Income Housing Coalition National Housing Law Project
National Alliance of HUD Tenants
Housing Assistance Council
Local Initiatives Support Corporation

Enterprise Community Partners

Action Housing (PA)

California Housing Partnership Corporation Chicago Community Development Corporation Chicago Rehab Network

Community Builders (MA)

Community Economic Development Assistance Corp (MA)

Community Service Society of New York Coalition on Housing and Homelessness in Ohio Coalition for Economic Survival (Los Angeles)

Community Development Law Center (Portland, OR) Housing Preservation Project (Minnesota) Neighborhood Reinvestment Corporation

New York Tenants and Neighbors

Stewards of Affordable Housing for the Future Texas Tenants Union

Urban Homesteading Assistance Board (NY) Emily Achtenberg (MA)

Preservation is a Crucial National Priority

Due to the recession that now grips our economy and the mortgage crisis that precipitated it, this legislation is needed today more than ever.

Continuing home foreclosures will shift many families from home-ownership to rental in a market where there is already a shortage of affordable rental housing for the poorest households. Many of the effected families will experience sharp declines in household assets and credit scores, but the increased demand is actually leading to higher rents and tighter credit screening in some markets, despite rising unemployment. At the same time, many cash-strapped states and local governments are reducing assistance to needy families. All of this leads to a heightened risk of homelessness for many families. Addressing this challenge begins with preserving existing affordable housing. As the Harvard report notes, "While efforts to create new units must continue, preserving the existing stock of good-quality, subsidized rental housing is even more important."[1]

The relatively high overall housing vacancy rate created by current economic conditions masks the critical mismatch between the nature of existing supply and unmet demand. A recent analysis conducted for HUD demonstrates that between 2005 and 2007 the number of units affordable to households at or below 50% of area median income fell by 7%, *or a loss of over 1.5 million homes*, while the number of units affordable to households with incomes of over 100% of area median grew by 34%.[2]

Further complicating this problem is the impact of the current economic crisis on the Low Income Housing Tax Credit. Uncertain profitability and investor flight from risk has created an unprecedented drop in LIHTC activity, dramatically reducing the creation of new affordable units.

At the heart of this legislation are new tools to protect residents and preserve affordability when assisted housing is refinanced, recapitalized, or when the underlying financing naturally matures. Thousands of apartments created under HUD mortgage subsidy programs are now at risk of conversion to non-affordable use when their mortgages mature. But unlike apartments with project-based Section 8 or apartments with HUD financing that is pre-paid by private owners, there are currently no provisions to extend the affordability of these units or to protect impacted residents. We are very pleased that the current draft includes provisions that would, at the owners' discretion, provide rental assistance for affected apartments, both for HUD-assisted and Rural Development Section 515 properties. These new preservation tools, in providing equal affordability protections to these apartments, are more cost-effective than other approaches to replace affordable apartments that are lost to conversion. Finally, improving preservation tools makes the rehabilitation of these properties less risky, leading to the creation of more construction jobs. According to recent studies in Oregon, the rehabilitation of 100 units creates over 150 new well-paying jobs.

There will be intense debate over the proposal to allow new owners to preserve the affordability of federally assisted property when current owners no longer wish to operate their properties as affordable housing. So long as existing owners are provided market value for their properties, we believe that new ownership dedicated to long term affordability will help ensure affordable rental housing at a time when so many families are homeless, at risk of homelessness, paying so much for housing that their food or health care needs are compromised, or living in substandard or overcrowded conditions. We pledge to protect the legitimate interests of owners to ensure that they receive fair and full sales prices to allow these properties to be preserved as affordable rental housing.

There will also be debate over the provision to allow residents to escrow their rents when properties are in disrepair. But let us be clear about what is proposed in the current draft: *all rents are to be paid,* but they will go into an escrow account or used for HUD-approved repairs when the Secretary determines serious violations of housing quality standards or housing program requirements. This is not an arbitrary and capricious standard. No one is suggesting that a tenant is allowed to avoid paying rent. The only parties who have something to fear from this provision are owners with serious property violations, which impact not only residents but the entire community.

We understand that some of these provisions are arguably already within the administrative jurisdiction of HUD, and that some of these actions may be taken without legislative action. While we are very pleased at the new focus on a balanced housing policy that re-emphasizes the importance of affordable rental housing, we are also mindful that any positive steps taken by this administration could be subsequently abandoned. We urge that these provisions be enacted as proposed.

We note that many members of the Committee recently expressed their support that recipients of housing subsidies should be American citizens. This is already the law of the land, and residents are currently required to certify compliance with this requirement. However, we are concerned about the impact on legal citizens created by any new citizenship documentation requirements for housing.

Many U.S. citizens who are senior citizens, African Americans, who live in rural areas, or who lack a high school diploma often do not have a birth certificate or passport in their possession. Obtaining such documents can be time-consuming and expensive, especially for those living far from their place of birth. In California it generally takes 10 to 12 weeks to get a birth certificate from the county office, and it can take six to eight months if the information submitted is not complete. A birth certificate can cost $5 to $23; a passport can cost up to $100.

Such requirements also create costs and delays for local governments. Since a similar requirement was implemented in Medicaid, Kansas reports a backlog of about 16,000 applications that are being delayed because of the difficulties complying with the new rule. New Medicaid processing requirements are projected to cost the state of Illinois $16 million to $19 million in the first year. Colorado allocated $2.7 million to comply with the requirement in the first year and now fears that it may not be enough. Recent Medicaid data from Alabama, Kansas, and Virginia show that the impacts of these requirements can be unpredictable:

- In *Virginia,* enrollment of Hispanic children actually rose 4.4 percent after the policy was implemented, while it fell sharply for white (4.3 percent) and African American (5 percent) children;
- In *Alabama,* Hispanic children make up 6 percent of those affected by the requirement but just 3 percent of those who lost coverage as a result;

- *Kansas* found that the enrollment decline under the requirement was 2.2 percent for Hispanic children, compared to 7.8 percent for white children and 9.1 percent for African American children.

We urge that Congress move with caution on any such new documentation requirements in order to avoid high compliance costs and disproportionate impacts on elderly and other legal program participants, with little potential impact on illegal use.

Finally, we support the additional titles for Section 202 elderly housing and for Section 515 rural housing administered by the Department of Agriculture. These proposed changes will provide important new tools to protect vital affordable rental housing for seniors and in rural areas that is at risk of deterioration or conversion, especially in high cost areas.

Federally Subsidized Housing is an Essential Housing Resource

The federally assisted housing rental stock is an especially important resource because it provides homes affordable to those with worst case housing needs at a time when housing affordability challenges are growing worse. The largest of these programs, the project-based Section 8 rental assistance program, provides affordable apartments for more than 1.3 million extremely low income households.

Our nation's most vulnerable families and seniors depend on quality affordable rental housing. According to a 2000 HUD survey, nearly 50% of federally subsidized housing is occupied by elderly or disabled persons. More than 77,000 veterans also depend on project-based affordable housing according to a December 2007 GAO report.

Federally subsidized housing serves nearly every community in the nation. The Trust's analysis shows that nearly 170,000 federally assisted apartments with contracts expiring over the next decade are located in the districts of the members of this committee, as shown in Attachment A. Many properties were constructed more than 30 years ago and are suffering from physical deterioration and are in need of significant capital improvements.

Current federal policies provide few incentives for the owner to retain the property's original use, compared to strong market incentives encouraging the owner to opt out of affordability requirements.

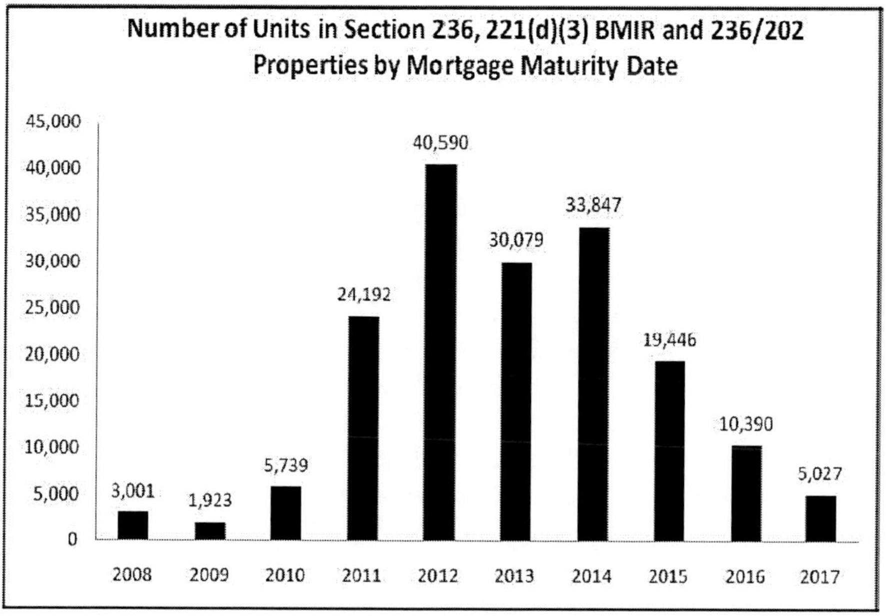

Over the next five years, contracts on more than 900,000 Section 8 units will expire. When a Section 8 contract expires, the owner can choose to opt out of the program, ending the obligation to maintain the housing as affordable. In addition, nearly 200,000 affordable apartments in properties with HUD subsidized mortgages will be at risk of conversion to non-affordable use when then mortgages mature over the next 10 years. Many of these apartments have project-based assistance included in the numbers above, but many receive no assistance but remain affordable to residents because of restrictions associated with the HUD-subsidized mortgages.

Federal government costs increase when an owner opt outs of a federal project-based rental assistance contract because the vouchers provided to protect eligible tenants from being displaced typically cost more—$1,000 more than the average project-based subsidy.

Current policies tend to limit the ability of preservation-minded owners to recapitalize, earn sufficient cash flow, and build a sustainable capital base. Owners, particularly nonprofit owners, are often not rewarded for taking risk. For example, HUD's current policy is to restrict the ability of nonprofit owners of federally regulated properties to take built up equity from the properties and use it for its housing mission. Current programs and regulations are fragmented, cumbersome, unpredictable and inconsistently applied.

Owners are frustrated with HUD's inability to promulgate meaningful regulations or to sensibly apply them. Here are but a few examples:

- Owners of Section 8 properties financed by State Housing Agencies are not entitled to mark their rents up to market, even though the market rents in the community may be higher than their current rents and the owner could use the funding to avoid operating at a deficit;
- HUD routinely terminates, rather than suspends, the Section 8 contracts on troubled properties, making it quite difficult for a new, mission minded owner to obtain debt and tax credits to repair the property;
- Current law requires that owners give notice to tenants and the federal government of a decision to opt out of a Section 8 contract or prepay the subsidized mortgage, but this information is not made publicly available. If preservation minded organizations knew which owners were planning to leave the federal programs, they could offer to purchase the property and preserve the apartments as affordable.

Preservation Works: Preserving Housing Is Cost Effective, Environmentally Responsible, and Is the Logical First Step in Solving Our Nation's Housing Dilemma

New construction alone will not produce enough affordable housing to meet the increasing demand. From 1995 to 2005, our nation lost nearly 1.4 million apartments with inflation-adjusted rents of $600 or less.[3] Although the low income housing tax credit program has typically generated approximately 100,000 affordable apartments each year, new construction does not add enough to the affordable rental stock to make up for lost units. In fact, for every new low-cost unit created each year, two are lost due to demolition, abandonment, or conversion to more expensive housing. Only when existing, subsidized and unsubsidized housing is preserved will building new affordable housing *add* to the affordable housing supply.

Over the past decade, state and local governments have increasingly devoted scarce resources, including low income housing tax credits, to preserve this housing. These tax credits have attracted billions of dollars in private sector investment in the rehabilitation of federally subsidized housing. Nearly all 50 states are now using low income housing tax credits to preserve existing affordable housing.

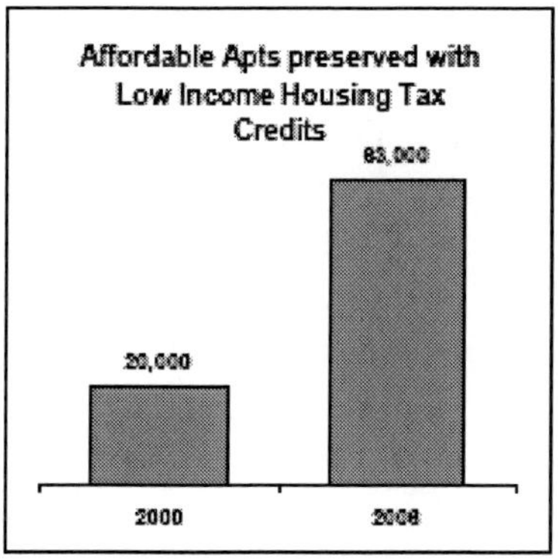

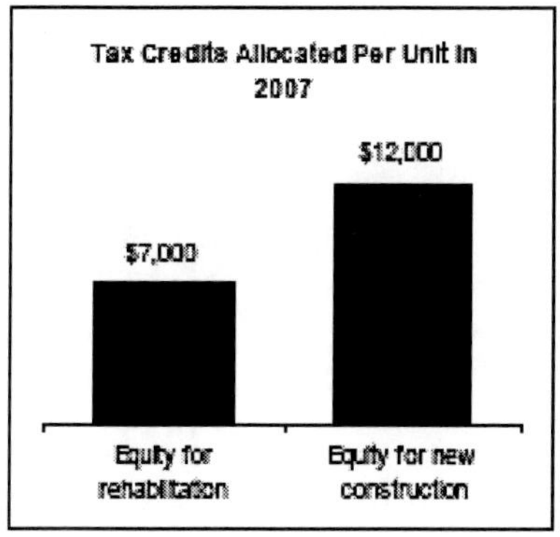

States' decisions to emphasize preservation are particularly sensible because preserving an existing home is significantly less expensive than constructing new affordable housing. Using data on the placement of tax credit equity from the National Council of State Housing Agencies, the Trust recently determined that it costs approximately 40% more to build a new affordable apartment than to preserve one in the same community. In more expensive communities, the cost of building new affordable housing is almost double preserving affordable housing in the same neighborhood.

Preserving existing affordable housing provides an opportunity to reinvest in and improve our communities and protect the historic investment made by the federal government. If we do not preserve and improve the millions of apartments that have been produced through these successful public-private partnerships, we will permanently lose our nation's most affordable homes. This will represent a squandering of billions of taxpayer dollars. Safeguarding this housing presents an opportunity to reinvest in and improve our communities.

It is also more energy efficient to preserve existing housing than it is to build new affordable housing where there is not an existing transportation infrastructure. Much of this housing serves as existing transit oriented development in our nation's cities. The National Housing Trust and Reconnecting America have identified federally assisted affordable housing located in close proximity to existing or proposed public transportation in 20 cities. *More than 250,000 federally assisted housing units in these cities are located within a half mile of rail or frequent bus transit. Approximately 63 percent of subsidized apartments near rail stations are covered by federal rental assistance contracts that expire before the end of 2012.*

Policymakers must act to ensure that this essential housing resource remains affordable to families and seniors. Preserving affordable housing near transit means more than simply saving a building—it means preserving meaningful transit opportunities for low-income families and seniors. Affordable housing located near transit allows families and seniors to live an affordable lifestyle in sustainable communities that offer access to employment, education, retail, and community opportunities.

Legislative Recommendations

Financing: Stabilize and dedicate increased public funding to long-term preservation ownership; provide adequate resources to assist residents of at-risk properties; expand public-private financing sources for preservation transactions. The Preservation Working Group recommends:

1. Providing tenant protections and alternatives to conversion for properties with expiring contracts or maturing mortgages;
2. Permiting owners to transfer project-based Section 8 to another property;
3. Utilizing all available preservation tools, such as up-front grants and retaining Section 8 for purchasers of distressed properties;
4. Enacting tax incentives to preserve affordability for qualified rental housing, as provided in H.R. 2887.

Incentives: Increase tax and regulatory incentives for sellers and owners of existing, affordable rental housing to encourage preservation, reduce speculation and maximize long-term affordability. The Preservation Working Group recommends the following incentives for long term stewardship of the existing inventory:

1. Enact enhancments to the Mark-to-Market program;
2. Protect state and local preservation laws against preemption;
3. Permit owners to project-base enhanced vouchers;
4. Ensure resident participation in the preservation process and full protections for tenants affected by converted properties; and
5. Affirm that HUD has a requirement to maximize preservation.

Information: The preservation database provision requires regular and timely release of property information that is already available in government databases. HUD already makes much of these data public, and is to be commended for these efforts. Unfortunately some of these data often appear too late to be useful for preservation, and often their appearance is irregular and the types of data that are available publically for each program vary considerably. For example, HUD's "Picture of Subsidized Housing," which provides a basic outline of its affordable rental housing programs, has not been updated for nine years. The draft bill provides a way to quickly combine the various databases going forward, through the use of unique property identifiers, so that preservation-oriented owners, developers, local governments, advocates, or federal agencies can quickly see the project-based assistance in place at any one property and in properties across the nation. As Secretary Donovan said in his testimony before this committee June 25, "a comprehensive database would help us do a far better job of preserving as many units as possible for the least amount of money."

Again, thank you for the opportunity to comment on this draft of affordable rental housing legislation. The National Housing Trust is eager to support this effort as it moves forward and looks forward to the formal introduction of this legislation.

I would be pleased to respond to any questions.

ATTACHMENT A

Privately Owned, Federally Assisted Affordable Housing in Financial Services Committee Members' Districts

Committee Member	Apts with Project-Based Contracts Expiring through FY2019
Rep. Frank, MA, *Chair*	3,277
Rep. Bachus, AL, *Rnk. Mem.*	641
Rep. Gary L. Ackerman, NY	1,015
Rep. John Adler, NJ	1,304
Rep. Joe Baca, CA	2,055
Rep. Michele Bachmann, MN	2,051
Rep. J. Gresham Barrett, SC	2,253

Rep. Melissa L. Bean, IL	1,954
Rep. Judy Biggert, IL	1,230
Rep. John Campbell, CA	1,205
Rep. Shelley Moore Capito, WV	2,520
Rep. Michael E. Capuano, MA	13,919
Rep. Andre Carson, IN	5,572
Rep. Michael N. Castle, DE	4,097
Rep. Travis Childers, MS	2,263
Rep. William Lacy Clay, MO	4,226
Rep. Emanuel Cleaver, MO	4,628
Rep. Joe Donnelly, IN	3,507
Rep. Steve Driehaus	4,931
Rep. Keith Ellison, MN	5,143
Rep. Bill Foster, IL	2,169
Rep. Scott Garrett, NJ	781
Rep. Jim Gerlach, PA	1,126
Rep. Alan Grayson, FL	822
Rep. Al Green, TX	2,448
Rep. Luis V. Gutierrez, IL	2,035
Rep. Jeb Hensarling, TX	854
Rep. Jim Himes, CT	3,461
Rep. Rubén Hinojosa, TX	1,669
Rep. Paul W. Hodes, NH	3,969
Rep. Lynn Jenkins, KS	2,479
Rep. Walter B. Jones, NC	1,213
Rep. Paul E. Kanjorski, PA	3,338
Rep. Mary Jo Kilroy	3,463
Rep. Peter King, NY	324
Rep. Ron Klein, FL	455
Rep. Suzanne Kosmas, FL	366
Rep. Leonard Lance, NJ	1,271
Rep. Christopher Lee, NY	3,000
Rep. Frank D. Lucas, OK	1,744
Rep. Stephen F. Lynch, MA	4,187

Rep. Dan Maffei, NY	3,622
Rep. Carolyn B. Maloney, NY	2,908
Rep. Donald A. Manzullo, IL	2,290
Rep. Kenny Marchant, TX	624
Rep. Carolyn McCarthy, NY	2,025
Rep. Kevin McCarthy, CA	1,001
Rep. Thaddeus McCotter, MI	2,421
Rep. Patrick T. McHenry, NC	1,145
Rep. Gregory W. Meeks, NY	2,698
Rep. Brad Miller, NC	2,579
Rep. Gary G. Miller, CA	410
Rep. Walt Minnick, ID	1,553
Rep. Dennis Moore, KS	2,330
Rep. Gwen Moore, WI	5,047
Rep. Randy Neugebauer, TX	1,388
Rep. Ron Paul, TX	752
Rep. Erik Paulsen, MN	2,607
Rep. Ed Perlmutter, CO	1,191
Rep. Gary Peters, MI	3,845
Rep. Bill Posey, FL	1,401
Rep. Tom Price, GA	285
Rep. Adam Putnam, FL	1,119
Rep. Edward R. Royce, CA	692
Rep. David Scott, GA	1,383
Rep. Brad Sherman, CA	2,540
Rep. Jackie Speier, CA	898
Rep. Nydia M. Velázquez, NY	4,973
Rep. Maxine Waters, CA	1,879
Rep. Melvin L. Watt, NC	2,608
Rep. Charles Wilson, OH	1,903
Total	169,082

TOBY HALLIDAY
VICE PRESIDENT

Toby Halliday is Vice President for Public Policy for the National Housing Trust (NHT). NHT engages in the preservation and revitalization of affordable rental housing through real estate development, lending, and public policy initiatives to better the quality of life for the families and elderly who live there. NHT has helped to save more than 22,000 affordable apartments in 41 states through technical assistance, real estate development, and lending activities. Since joining the Trust in early 2008, Toby has worked with other supporters of affordable rental housing to promote policy changes at HUD and in Congress to facilitate the preservation and improvement of affordable rental housing. Mr. Halliday is the moderator of the National Preservation Working Group.

Prior to joining NHT, Mr. Halliday was Program Director for preservation of affordable housing at the Local Initiatives Support Corporation (LISC). During his five year tenure, LISC committed $69 million in financing and provided technical support to over 100 preservation projects and over 12,500 affordable homes. Previously Toby managed loans and technical assistance for rural community development efforts and administered federal grants and technical assistance for the reuse of closed U.S. military facilities.

End Notes

[1] Joint Center for Housing Studies. (2008).*America's Rental Housing: The Key to a Balanced National Policy*. Cambridge: Joint Center for Housing Studies of Harvard University, p. 22.

[2] Eggers, F.J. & Moumen, F. (2009, June). *American Housing Survey: Rental Housing Dynamics: 2005-2007*. Prepared for U.S. Department of Housing and Urban Development Office of Policy Development and Research. Bethesda, MD: Econometrica, Inc.

[3] Joint Center for Housing Studies. (2008). *America's Rental Housing: The Key to a Balanced National Policy*. Cambridge: Joint Center for Housing Studies of Harvard University.

In: HUD-Assisted Housing Preservation ISBN: 978-1-61324-856-0
Editors: J. Moran and A. Davies

Chapter 4

Statement of Ricky Leung, Treasurer, National Alliance of HUD Tenants, Before the Subcommittee on Housing and Community Opportunity, Hearing on "Affordable Housing Preservation and Protection of Tenants"*

July 15, 2009

On behalf of the National Alliance of HUD Tenants (NAHT), I want to thank Chairwoman Waters, Ranking Member Bachus, and members of the Subcommittee for inviting our testimony today. My name is Ricky Leung. I am an architect by profession and a tenant in project-based Section 8 housing; the President of the Cherry Street Tenant Association in the Lower East Side of Manhattan; and the elected Treasurer of the NAHT Board. I also work closely with NAHT's New York affiliates, New York Tenants and Neighbors, the Urban Homesteading Assistance Board (UHAB), and Good Ole Lower East Side (GOLES).

NAHT is the national tenant union representing the 1.7 million families who live in privately-owned, HUD assisted multifamily housing, including the

* This is an edited, reformatted and augmented version of a Statement given by Ricky Leung, Treasurer, National Alliance of HUD Tenants, Before the Subcommittee on Housing and Community Opportunity, Hearing on "Affordable Housing Preservation and Protection of Tenants", on July 15, 2009.

1.3 million families, elderly and disabled people in apartments receiving project-based Section 8 assistance. The elected NAHT Board represents a membership including voting member tenant groups and areawide coalitions in 23 states.

Since Congress ended the Title VI Preservation Program in 1996, the nation has lost at least 360,000 units of affordable low income housing, through owner conversion to high market rents and/or voucherization by HUD. The Draft Preservation Bill prepared by Committee staff represents a tremendous step toward halting this loss. We commend Chairman Frank and Chairwoman Waters for including virtually all of NAHT's priority concerns in the Draft Bill, especially the no-cost First Right of Purchase in Section 103.

We also thank Representative Velasquez, who represents my District in Manhattan, for filing HR 44, the Troubled Housing reforms now incorporated in Title IV of the Draft Bill. In 1994, Congress gave HUD "flexible authority" to voucher out troubled housing, with little oversight. The nation has since lost 120,000 formerly subsidized apartments through HUD policy decisions. Today, 16,000 families in 122 substandard apartment complexes face foreclosure in New York City alone. We applaud Representative Velasquez, Chairman Frank and Chairwoman Waters for including these NAHT priorities in the Draft Bill.

NAHT testified and commented on the 2008 Discussion Draft of this bill. In the revised Draft, we appreciate that Committee staff have made major improvements to the Right to Purchase section, as well as to Section 503 regarding HUD approved prepayments, and added important provisions for HUD held and HUD owned buildings in a new Section 108. About 90% of the Bill has consensus support among the major stakeholders, including several NAHT priorities (all of HR 44 and other Troubled Housing reforms; reform and extension of Enhanced Vouchers for all expiring units; Project Based Enhanced Vouchers; and conversion of Rent Supplement and RAP contracts to Section 8). There is also consensus support for Section 513, the Tenant Technical Assistance provision, which is identical to the language adopted unanimously in HR 3965 in October 2007. We thank Representative Green, Chairman Frank and Ranking Members Bachus and Capito for their leadership on this provision.

Accordingly, my remarks today focus on NAHT's highest priorities for this legislation, namely the Federal First Right of Purchase (Section 103) and Tenant Empowerment provisions (Sections 303, 304 and 305). These priorities have been endorsed by the National Preservation Working Group, but have not been supported by all stakeholders.

Federal First Right of Purchase Will Save Our Homes

I am honored to represent NAHT before you today. For 30 years, I have grown up in the 488 unit Cherry Street Apartment complex in a Section 8 apartment with my two aging parents, whose stable jobs in the garment industry were largely wiped out after 9/11. Cherry Street has provided a secure home for our family, which I largely support while working as an apprentice architect in Manhattan. Neither my parents nor I would be able to survive long paying full rent in the overheated Manhattan market.

The other 487 families in the Cherry Street community are working families, professionals and retirees; old, young, and in between; African American, Caucasian, Asian-American and Latino. We are the diverse New York working and middle class, a microcosm of the City and of the nation. As President of the Cherry Street Tenants Association for the past eight years, I have worked to help our community sustain and thrive in the face of increasing threats from a super hot real estate market.

In 2003, our project-based Section 8 contract was set to expire again after several one year extensions. We were fearful and uncertain what would be the fate of our community, given rapid gentrification and mega development projects in the Lower East Side. Our Tenant Association persuaded our owner to renew under the Mark Up to Market Program, but only for five years. After I testified before the Committee in 2008, our building was sold to a "predatory equity" investor for $177 million –more than $360,000 per apartment—who renewed the Section 8 contract for another five years. The new owner will face the same decision of whether or not to renew in three years. Next time around, we are not so certain he will renew: he can likely make far more money converting to speculative rents on unsubsidized units or converting to condominiums.

Passage of a first right of purchase would at least give our tenant association and the city a fighting chance to save our homes.

By itself, the First Right of Purchase provision would not add to federal costs. It would simply allow a City agency, acting alone or on behalf of a nonprofit or tenant organization, to purchase a property at risk of conversion to market housing during a six month window of time, during the owner's One Year Notice period already required by federal law. A preservation purchaser would use current federal subsidy programs such as Mark Up to Market, Low Income Housing Tax Credits, city and state capital grants or loans, the National Housing Trust Fund, Stimulus Bill funds and new federal preservation grants to buy the property at full market value, while preserving affordable housing for future and current tenants. Agencies awarding funds would ensure that repair needs are met to protect tenants and the buildings.

If a viable purchase plan cannot be assembled in the required time frame, the owner would be free to opt out. In that case, the Draft Bill's provisions for Enhanced Vouchers for all current tenants (including Expiring Mortgage units) would apply.

The Right of First Purchase framework is similar to the Title II/VI Preservation program, which preserved 90,000 at-risk apartments between 1988 and 1996. Of these, 30,000 apartments were purchased by nonprofit or tenant organizations. Tenants in my building deserve the same opportunity.

New York City is Losing Affordable Housing at an Alarming Rate

Tenants' fears that owners might opt out are unfortunately well founded. As of the end of 2006, fully 27% of New York City's original 119,785 units of privately-owned, subsidized housing have been lost since 1990, and another 18% (21,561 total) were threatened with subsidy loss, according to the Community Services Society (CSS).1 *Of the 32,422 units lost so far, 17,911 were in federally subsidized apartments that could have been saved if a First Right of Purchase were in place*. Needless to say, the City of New York is not building new housing affordable to low income families at anywhere near this rate.

Since 9/11, the rate of housing loss has spiked dramatically: more than 2/3 of the units lost overall since 1990 have converted since 2001. Mitchell-Lama buildings with older, non-Section rent subsidy programs (Rent Supplement and RAP, which are not eligible for Mark Up to Market) have opted out at an alarming rate. By 2004, these trends had spread from high market areas such as the Upper West Side to "medium" market areas in the City, including lower rent areas of Manhattan and the Bronx. In my neighborhood, Land's End I converted to the market rents in 2004. In 2007, the proposed conversion of the 6,000 unit Starrett City complex—the nation's largest HUD subsidized development—was only the most visible example of a much deeper crisis in our city. The new crisis in expiring 40 year HUD mortgages will only accelerate this loss.

In the wake of the traumas inflicted on New York City in 2001, the loss of more than 54,000 affordable housing units is a crisis which we can neither bear nor ignore. The people of our city are still reeling from the after shocks of 9/11. Cherry Street and other subsidized housing developments are home to many of the police, firefighters and health service workers who performed heroically after the 9/11 attacks, as well as many low income and elderly people who simply have no options in the high rental market of New York City.

Homeland security begins with a home. Adoption of a First Right of Purchase is urgently needed to preserve the estimated 20,000 federally subsidized apartments at immediate risk in New York City alone.

Predatory Investors are Driving up Rents and Destroying Affordable Housing

Since 9/11, the destruction of affordable housing has been fueled by an unprecedented surge of speculative investment by large, international private equity firms taking advantage of the declining dollar and market conditions in New York. A stone's throw from the World Trade Center, Independence Plaza was lost to a predatory investor who converted to high rent housing in 2004. Since then, 13,000 subsidized apartments have been acquired and deregulated by three predatory equity firms in New York City alone, with no end in sight.

For example, Cammeby's International, a private equity firm based in the Middle East, purchased 10 and 210 Stanton Street in the Lower East Side, not far from where I live, along with 10 other developments totaling 7,458 apartments in New York City. In Harlem, another investor sold 4,000 units of state and HUD subsidized housing for $300 million ($79,000 per unit) in May 2005, who then flipped them to a second investment fund managed by Morgan Stanley, for almost $1 billion ($250,000 per unit) in 2007. The new owner tripled the debt service in a two year period, creating tremendous pressure to replace low income people with higher rent paying tenants. My own building, Cherry Street, has now joined the list of predatory equity targets with its sale at $360,000 per unit last year.

City and state agencies in New York have stepped in where they can to review and reject sales of subsidized housing where speculative purchase prices appear unsupportable, but their authority is limited. With pressure from Rep. Velasquez, HUD Secretary Jackson did block the sale at Starrett City for $220,000 per unit. But not all at-risk properties have HUD mortgages that allow HUD to do this, and HUD has rarely rejected a sale.[2] *A First Right of Purchase would provide an additional tool to local governments to remove at-*

risk buildings from the speculative market spiral entirely, with a one time purchase and transfer to socially responsible ownership.

Deregulation Has Resulted in Uncontrolled Speculation and the Loss of Housing

The explosion of predatory equity speculation in New York's subsidized housing stock is echoed in other high market areas from Boston to San Francisco, Atlanta to Los Angeles, and will soon spread to gentrifying neighborhoods across the country. It is one byproduct of the deregulation of federally subsidized housing since 1996. As in the single family mortgage industry, deregulation and speculation in subsidized multifamily housing have already had hugely negative consequences for affordable housing, low income families and communities.

Deregulation is a strategy that has failed in the mortgage lending, energy, telecommunications, banking, and airline industries in the US and in countries around the globe. It is a failure in the subsidized housing industry as well. It is time to push back with judicious, moderate regulation to save affordable rental housing, as the Committee has recommended for the single family mortgage and banking industries.

The predatory equity crisis poses new challenges for all of us. NAHT appreciates the Committee's leadership in addressing the need for new regulatory controls, such as the language protecting tenants and affordable rental housing in the TARP legislation, and Rep. Velasquez' proposals for a Multifamily Housing Preservation Program, which are currently under review by the Treasury Department and HUD. The First Right of Purchase is one more critical regulatory tool which residents and cities need in our arsenal to save our homes.

There is ample precedent for the limited, no-cost regulatory tool of the First Right of Purchase. *Besides Title VI, for 20 years Congress has provided a Right of Purchase in the federally subsidized Rural Housing sector, which has worked to preserve this stock from conversion to high market rents.*[3] *In addition, since 1996 several states, including Illinois, Rhode Island, and Maine have adopted First Right of Purchase statutes.*

New York Courts Nullified Local Law 79 Due to Preemption, Not Constitutional Concerns, and Called for Action by Other Levels of Government

In New York City, tenants won Local Law 79, which enacted a First Right of Purchase in the City, based on these statewide models. We are aware that HUD Secretary Donovan expressed reservations about the Right of First Purchase at the Committee hearing on June 25, 2009. The Secretary alluded to "constitutional" and other objections which were raised by landlord groups and the City of New York in state court litigation which ultimately struck down Local Law 79. He suggested that the Committee explore these constitutional issues and proceed cautiously before adopting this regulatory tool.

In response, it is important to note that the New York state trial court (upheld upon appeal) struck down Local Law 79 due to concerns about preemption conflicts with state and federal laws, not because of any constitutional "taking" concerns, which the court did not address. Obviously, establishing a national Right of First Purchase, or altering the federal Notice laws, will not present any federal "preemption" problems. In fact, the New York Court wrote that "the recent sales and proposed sales of major assisted rental housing complexes in this City and the likely devastating impact of those sales on low and moderate-income residents of New York may and should function as a wake-up call for the need for immediate action" by other levels of government. We are attaching to our testimony a recent memorandum prepared by the National Housing Law Project, highlighting these points and addressing the constitutionality of Section 103.

We agree with Secretary Donovan that the Right of First Purchase provision in the bill should be carefully crafted to avoid successful constitutional challenges, by for example ensuring that there is no unwarranted delay in the exercise of a city's right to purchase and that landlords receive full market compensation for any sale. The language in Section 103 of the Draft Bill meets those tests, and improves on the Title II and VI programs in that respect.

On the question of federal preemption, the New York Court referred to Section 232 of the now-defunct Title VI program, which expressly preempts state or local laws that regulate rents in buildings that were once eligible for Title VI. Since the original purpose of Section 232—to ensure that appraisals under Title VI reflected unrestricted market value, regardless of local rent control laws—is no longer applicable, this archaic provision should be clarified, limited only to properties that executed a Title VI Plan.

More broadly, there is no sound reason for Congress to block state and local governments from protecting their own communities, or to do more to preserve affordable housing or to protect tenants than the federal government if they wish. Section 107 of the Draft Bill addresses this concern.

The First Right of Purchase Will Save Money with Greater Benefits for at-Risk Families

Congress dismantled Title VI in 1996 due to concerns about excessive costs. But *the federal costs of the current "unregulated" owner choice system usually match or exceed the cost of Title VI, but with none of the benefits.*

Today, an owner who "opts out" receives Enhanced Section 8 Vouchers which pay the full market rent for assisted units, but with no HUD oversight. An owner who chooses to renew under Mark Up to Market likewise is paid full market rents by HUD, for 5 to 20 years, with no requirement to make needed repairs. Either way, HUD pays out a full market rent in subsidies equivalent to what was formerly paid out under Title VI, but with none of the offsetting benefits. *Under Title VI, residents and HUD negotiated major repair programs, permanent affordability, and transfers to nonprofit purchasers and tenant organizations; none of these are required by HUD under either Enhanced Vouchers or Mark Up to Market.*

In fact, short term extensions under Mark Up to Market of five years leave residents and HUD at continued risk that owners will opt out down the road, as is happening in my building in the Lower East Side. *As long as owners have an unrestricted choice to opt out of HUD programs, they will be able to leverage ever-increasing subsidy commitments from HUD-- which residents and communities will doubtless support--since the alternative of losing affordable housing is unacceptable.* Owners who opt out likewise trigger Enhanced Voucher costs at least the same or higher the subsidy costs in previously regulated developments. In speculative markets like New York, HUD often pays out artificially inflated subsidies—in effect, taxpayer financed windfall profits--that in turn contribute to the speculative spiral in our neighborhoods, with no public benefits other than preservation of Section 8 housing.

A First Right of Purchase will save money in the long run by removing subsidized developments from this speculative spiral, lessening owner windfalls, and ensuring that Congress receives guaranteed benefits on its investment of any federal funds such as Section 8 or the National Housing Trust Fund. Implementing the First Right of Purchase in New York would help stabilize and pull back residential real estate markets from speculative pressures that ramp up prices above true values.

Section 103 Will Save Housing Threatened by Expiring Mortgages and Other Risks

While Mark Up to Market may have slowed the loss of housing since 2000 in some regions, it has by no means stopped it. In addition to the challenges of speculation in high market areas, tenants are now threatened by the rapid growth of "expiring 40 year mortgages" across the nation, a problem that emerged in 2007 and will accelerate through at least 2015. The Federal First Right to Purchase, coupled with the Project Based Enhanced Voucher provision and other incentives in the Draft Bill, will give tenants and communities the tools they need to save these and other at-risk buildings.

In June 2008, the Committee heard about the struggle of Lincoln Place tenants in *Venice, California* against AIMCO, the world's largest residential Real Estate Investment Trust (REIT) and a major speculator in HUD housing. Lincoln Place could have been saved had a First Right of Purchase been in place at the time.

The same can be said about many other AIMCO buildings. For example, take Northwest Terrace and Northlake Terrace in *Dallas*, two AIMCO buildings that once provided a racially integrated community for 472 families. In 1996, the tenants picked a nonprofit to buy both developments under Title VI, but the program ended before the sale could go through. AIMCO later indicated they would consider selling to a nonprofit, but they reneged and sold to another predatory investor in 2000. Conditions deteriorated, and rents skyrocketed 60-75% as the new owner planned to flip the land for luxury townhouse development. The property has since been demolished. This tragedy could have been avoided had a First Right of Purchase been in place.

In Boston, First Realty Management, which owns several thousand apartments refinanced in the early 1990's with equity take-out loans netting $46 million for the owners, converted the 540 unit High Point Village complex in August 2006, when the original HUD 40 year mortgage expired.

The owner and his family invested only $120,000 in 1966, netting more than $90 million in windfall profits by 2006 paid largely by steadily escalating Section 8 subsidies. The owner spurned appeals to at least preserve 320 apartments as Section 8 housing, opting out instead. FRM is now systematically converting its entire portfolio, more than 2,000 apartments statewide, when they reach the end of their 40 year mortgage term. The City of Boston could have exercised a First Right of Purchase to remove High Point from the speculative market to preserve affordable housing and racial diversity.

In *Hawaii*, the Right of Purchase, along with the revised Section 503 of the Draft Bill, would have helped preserve affordability at Kukui Gardens, an 850 unit complex being converted to mostly market housing by the nonprofit owner. Hawaii has the second highest rate of Section 8 opt outs in the country, according to the Government Accounting Office (GAO)[4]. Section 503 would tighten HUD approval requirements for prepayment by nonprofit owners, to help avoid housing losses like Kukui in the future.

Tenant Empowerment Provisions Essential

NAHT's second priority is the Tenant Empowerment measures included in Title III of the Draft Bill. Along with the urgently needed reactivation of Section 514 funds required by Section 601, these no-cost measures will empower tenants to participate as full partners with HUD to improve and save their homes. These tools will enable tenants to utilize the First Right of Purchase to save at-risk buildings, as NAHT affiliates helped preserve 90,000 apartments under Title II and VI Preservation. They also complement the Troubled Housing reform measures in Title IV of the Draft Bill. [5]

Particularly important are provisions to give tenants Access to Information regarding project budgets and ownership and substandard housing (Section 305 and 306), Third Party Beneficiary Status in HUD contracts with owners (Section 304), and Rent Withholding procedures for substandard housing (Section 303).

Access to Information (Section 305 and 601). The value of transparency regarding use of taxpayer subsidies should be self evident. Project ownership and budget information can help tenants spot waste, fraud and abuse in the use of HUD money in the buildings where we live. Tenants have the greatest stake, and the first hand knowledge, to make sure that public subsidies are used well—these are our homes. *Only owners and managers who fail to provide quality service and/or have something to hide should raise any objection to empowering tenants with this information.*

Recently in New York City tenants had a major victory in preserving at risk housing thanks to our ability to get access to detailed financial information with the help of city and state agencies—including blind rent rolls, operating budgets and proposed sale prices. This information has aided tenants and advocates in getting regulatory agencies to reject speculative sales of subsidized projects at Starrett City and 1520 Sedgwick, known as the "Birth of Hip Hop" building in the Bronx. Tenants are now pursuing resident ownership at 1520 Sedgwick.

Tenants in other parts of the country deserve the same access to information which has empowered residents in New York without any discernable harm to owners.

HUD does not now make available project budget information under the Freedom of Information Act (FOIA), outside of a short period when owners apply for rent increases. Amazingly, HUD also refuses to provide REAC inspection scores to "failed" buildings that have been referred to HUD's Enforcement Center—precisely the buildings where tenant cooperation with HUD should be encouraged the most. Worse, in 2003 former HUD Deputy Secretary Bernardi adopted a controversial policy effectively withholding information from FOIA requests that involve "current or former senior HUD management officials" or ask "questions about HUD's policies or the performance of departmental responsibilities," leaving it up to local staff to flag "controversial" FOIA requests. The outgoing Administration further weakened the FOIA with 11th hour regulations in October 2008 that impose steep fees and other obstacles to tenants seeking basic information. One result: in October 2008, HUD declined a request for an approved Mark to Market plan to a nonprofit Rhode Island tenant assistance group unless the tenants paid HUD $5,800 to assemble a copy of the Plan, even though HUD's own regulations require release of the Plan to the tenants and their representatives! Clear direction by Congress is required to help the new Administration reverse these now institutionalized policies.

Particularly where public subsidies are concerned, tenants and the public generally should know where our tax dollars are going. Subsidy contracts with owners should not be treated as a secret compact of private information beyond public scrutiny. Claims that making project budgets available to tenants will discourage investment and inhibit the effectiveness of preservation owners are contrary to the experience in areas where this information is available from local governments. In fact, as Sedgwick and Starrett City have shown, making information available to the public will enable tenants to encourage, not discourage, investment by preservation purchasers.

Rent Withholding (Section 303). This proposal would allow tenants to withhold rent when there are serious violations of housing quality standards and trigger HUD to withhold as well. It also provides that HUD will conduct an inspection or management review when requested by the local government or a petition signed by not less than 10% of the tenants. This proposal is based on language which passed the House in 1993 or was included in a Senate Floor Managers Amendment, but which was not adopted in final legislation. NAHT has submitted technical amendments to refine Section 303.

Many states allow rent withholding for serious substandard conditions; states like Massachusetts or Ohio report no problems of frivolous litigation, serious controversy or abuse. But Alabama, North Carolina, South Carolina, Louisiana, Georgia, Missouri, Colorado, Oklahoma and Texas are among the states that do not have this right. HUD receivership authority is rarely used and inaccessible to most tenants. *Rent withholding creates a strong incentive for the owner to repair, and can help save buildings before they deteriorate. Section 303 is a natural complement to Title IV and will enlist tenants as partners with HUD in improving Troubled Housing.*

Third Party Beneficiary Status (Section 304). This proposal would establish tenants and tenant associations as third party beneficiaries in HUD contracts affecting their property. Tenants are listed as third party beneficiaries in Mark-to-Market Use agreements, but not in the Section 8 contract or any other Mark-to-Market documents, such as the Rehab Escrow Deposit Agreement or Mark-to-Market Restructuring Commitments. *HUD is often slow or too late in enforcing these contracts, leaving tenants to suffer. Adding tenants as third party beneficiaries would give us standing to enforce the contracts.*

One example will illustrate why this proposal is needed. The Texas Tenants Union reports that there is a 100 unit property in Longview, TX called the Jerusalem Apartments that completed HUD's Mark-to-Market (M2M) program in November 2001. The M2M plan called for $83,750 to be spent from the Rehab Escrow Account in the first year for new hot water heaters, exterior painting and carpentry, repairs to the water and sewer lines, and other repairs. Another $48,000 was supposed to be spent from the Reserve Account in the first year to begin replacing windows, furnaces, and appliances. More than two years after M2M approval, none of the improvements had begun. By the fall of 2006, HUD terminated the Section 8 contract and displaced all the families, senior citizens, and disabled tenants. HUD proceeded to foreclose on the property in the fall of 2007, and has scheduled at least three auctions to sell the property, which of course, is now without subsidies. If the tenants had been able to withhold rent early on, or been a party to the contracts, there likely would have been a better outcome.

Action Need to Make Resources Available to Empower Tenants

NAHT strongly supports Section 513, which would direct HUD to provide $10 million annually under Section 514 of MAHRAA which Congress has authorized since 1997 but HUD has not spent since 2002. Sponsored by Rep. Al Green, this language was adopted with a strong bipartisan consensus by the full Committee in October 2007 as part of the Mark to Market Reform bill, now incorporated in the Draft bill.

Tenants urgently need the resources Section 513 would provide in order to cope with a variety of preservation challenges, including the growth of expiring 40 year mortgages, troubled housing, and predatory equity. Despite the Committee's vote in October 2007, HUD has yet to provide these resources, although HUD's FY2010 Appropriations request includes $10 million for Section 514 in the project-based Section 8 account. HUD should be able to make funds available by October 2009.

It is critical for the Committee to retain Section 513 in the Preservation Bill, and to encourage HUD to implement the Committee's policy directives in the interim. An Interagency Agreement between HUD and the Corporation for National Service or similar federal agency, as provided in Section 513, is the only and most cost effective way to get resources out to the field during 2009. Similarly, it is important for HUD to implement a new grant program based on performance based contracts for eligible incurred costs, not the unworkable "fee for activity" model proposed for the new "TRIO" grant program planned by HUD staff in 2007, and to ensure that qualified locally based intermediaries get priority for grant funds. So far, HUD has not indicated support for these key provisions in Section 513.

Similarly, it is important for the Committee to urge HUD to heed the recommendations of the Alternative Management Control Review (AMCR), HUD's internal report generated by audits of earlier Section 514 programs. The AMCR recommended that new programs be administered by the Office of Grant Administration in the Office of Housing, rather than by OAHP, which had failed in its oversight of earlier programs. The AMCR further recommended that the OGA/OH be assigned three program staff to provide better oversight through Cooperative Grant Agreements. We strongly support these recommendations and ask the Committee to urge HUD to implement them, along with the policies outlined in Section 513.

NAHT and its local affiliates have the strongest stake in making sure the new program works to empower tenants. We ask the Committee's continued support to make sure that HUD adopts our recommendations to get resources out in the most timely, cost effective and effective manner.

****

In summary, we urge the Committee to retain the critical provisions for a First Right of Purchase and Tenant Empowerment. The Committee has crafted an exciting and comprehensive program that will sustain our homes for decades to come.

We would be happy to provide more information to the Committee upon request. Thank you for developing this legislation and allowing NAHT to submit its views.

MEMORANDUM

TO:	Subcommittee on Housing and Community Opportunity, House Financial Services Committee
FROM:	James Grow and Adam Cowing, National Housing Law Project
RE:	Proposed Federal First Right of Purchase
DATE:	July 13, 2009

The Federal First Right of Purchase Does not Amount to an Unconstitutional Taking

The Fifth Amendment requires that "private property [shall not] be taken for public use, without just compensation." Though there is no clear precedent that the proposed right of purchase would even constitute a "taking," the proposed federal first right of purchase satisfies the Fifth Amendment because it provides just compensation and furthers a valid public purpose.

- *The bill's purpose – to preserve affordable housing – is a public use.* The public use requirement has been interpreted broadly by the

Supreme Court. The judiciary's role in judging public use is narrow and should be restrained "unless the use be palpably without reasonable foundation." *Hawaii Hous. Auth. v. Midkiff*, 104 S. Ct. 2321, 2329 (1984). Further, property taken need not be put into use for the general public, nor must it be held by public entities. The "mere fact that property... is transferred... to private beneficiaries does not condemn that taking as having only a private purpose." *Kelo v. City of New London*, 545 U.S. 469, 482 (2005) (citing *Midkiff*, 104 S. Ct. at 2331).

- *The proposed right of purchase specifically requires just compensation.* Takings analysis requires two steps: determining whether a taking has occurred and, if so, whether just compensation has been provided. Just compensation obviates the need to address the first requirement, since the Fifth Amendment does not prohibit the taking of property, only the taking of property without just compensation. The proposed bill requires that owners receive fair market value if a property is sold (sec. 103(d)(3)(B)), which the Supreme Court has held satisfies the just compensation requirement of the Fifth Amendment. *Palazzolo v. Rhode Island*, 533 U.S. 606 (2001). Nor is there any temporary takings issue since the proposed bill permits an owner to convert at the end of the original notice period if the qualified preservation purchaser does not purchase the property (sec. 103(b)) – the same date upon which the owner could otherwise convert.
- *Precedent:* The proposed federal right of purchase is analogous to 42 U.S.C. § 1472(c), which in 1988 established a purchase right for Rural Development rental housing facing prepayment. This law has been upheld in court, against claims that it violated due process and was an unconstitutional taking. *Parkridge Investors v. Farmers Home Admin.*, 13 F.3d 1192 (8th Cir. 1994); *Lifgren v. Yeutter*, 767 Fed. Supp. 1473 (D.Minn. 1991) (deciding only the takings issue).

HUD's Position on a Federal First Right of Purchase

When asked about HUD's position on the federal right of purchase (question from Rep. Maxine Waters, June 25, 2009, Committee Hearing), Secretary Donovan stated his opinion that a legislative right to purchase must be "crafted very carefully," and is not the most important tool for preserving affordable housing.

Based upon his experience in New York City, the Secretary cited two levels of complex legal issues, which should "be looked into very carefully" because they might engender burdensome litigation: constitutional issues and state level issues. Since only constitutional issues are relevant to Congress' evaluation of possible legal impediments to a *federal* law, the inquiry here should focus upon any issues posed by the takings doctrine and the Supremacy Clause. While takings claims might be filed, they would be difficult to sustain under the authorities previously cited, and none was decided in New York. Concerning the Supremacy Clause, the Secretary's experience involved a local right of purchase law that was challenged and eventually invalidated as impliedly preempted by federal law. *Mother Zion Tenant Ass'n v. Donovan*, 865 N.Y.S.2d 64 (2008). Whatever the merits of the state court's federal preemption ruling, no such problem is presented here, for two reasons. First, a *federal* right of purchase affirmatively establishes federal policy, which must be given effect under the Supremacy Clause. Second, the proposed bill expressly clarifies that state and local preservation laws are not preempted (sec. 107(d)). The Secretary also stated that litigation challenging the New York City law disrupted preservation efforts, but this assertion or its relevance to the proposed federal policy cannot be evaluated without more facts

Secretary Donovan also expressed his belief that the federal right of purchase is not the most effective tool for preservation, stating that "carrots" are more important than "sticks" in preserving affordable housing. To be sure, incentives are of critical importance, and the proposed bill includes many such carrots, none of which are excluded in favor of creating a right to purchase. Although the federal government has provided many preservation incentives, an additional tool is necessary to preserve the value of those investments where owners reject incentives. We submit that the right to purchase at market value properly balances the owner's financial interest with the need to preserve affordable homes.

End Notes

[1] The full CSS report is available on line at http://www.cssny.org/pdfs/Closing_the_ Door_ 2007_Report.pdf.

[2] One measure sought by NAHT and included in the Preservation Working Group proposals is a provision mandating that HUD preserve at risk housing when it has discretion to do so. This

brief proposal would nonetheless be important to redress the many ways that HUD officials have acted in a manner which undermines, rather than preserves, affordable housing. We were unable to find this proposal in the Draft Bill; since it should be noncontroversial among the HUD stakeholders, we recommend its inclusion in the final bill.

[3] 42 U.S.C. Sec. 1472 (c).

[4] "Project Based Rental Assistance," GAO-07-290, April 2007.

[5] NAHT has also made recommendations to increase tenant involvement and minimize abuse in the Section 202 provisions authorizing transfer of project-based Section 8 contracts from one building to another.

In: HUD-Assisted Housing Preservation
Editors: J. Moran and A. Davies
ISBN: 978-1-61324-856-0

Chapter 5

TESTIMONY OF THE INSTITUTE FOR RESPONSIBLE HOUSING PRESERVATION PRESENTED BY SARAH METHERELL, VICE PRESIDENT, STEADFAST COMPANIES FINANCIAL SERVICES COMMITTEE SUBCOMMITTEE ON HOUSING AND COMMUNITY OPPORTUNITY U.S. HOUSE OF REPRESENTATIVES HEARING ON AFFORDABLE HOUSING PRESERVATION*

July 15, 2009

Madam Chairman. Thank you for inviting me to testify on the important topic of affordable housing preservation. My name is Sarah Metherell. I am Vice President of Acquisitions for Steadfast Residential Properties which is based in Newport Beach, CA. Steadfast Residential is involved in the

---

* This is an edited, reformatted and augmented version of a Testimony of the Institute for Responsible Housing Preservation Presented by Sarah Metherell Vice President, Steadfast Companies Financial Services Committee Subcommittee on Housing and Community Opportunity U.S. House pf Representatives Hearing on Affordable Housing Preservatio, on July 15, 2009.

acquisition, rehabilitation and preservation of federally assisted multifamily affordable housing properties. We own and manage approximately 15,000 apartments in 18 states, concentrated primarily in California and the Western United States. Nearly all of our properties receive some form of federal assistance including low income housing tax credits and project based Section 8.

I am here today in my capacity as Vice President of the Institute for Responsible Housing Preservation ("IRHP"). Since 1989 IRHP has represented owners and managers of federally assisted multifamily properties on preservation issues including advocating for legislative and regulatory changes for preservation policies and providing educational seminars on preserving affordable housing. IRHP members worked with this committee and HUD in structuring and closing the first Section 236 "de-coupling" preservation transactions in 1998. More than 800 Section 236 properties – approximately 80,000 units – have been substantially rehabbed and preserved as affordable housing over the past 11 years using the de-coupling program. In his testimony before the Financial Services Committee two weeks ago, HUD Secretary Shaun Donovan recognized the de-coupling program as one of HUD's premier and successful preservation initiatives.

Madam Chairman, as you know well, even with the success of the 236 de-coupling transactions, there is more work to be done in preserving the existing HUD multifamily portfolio. No one questions the need for affordable housing. Various private and public studies prove that. Yet, notwithstanding the benefits and proven success of the Section 236 de-coupling preservation program HUD has not taken the lessons learned from this initiative and applied them beyond the Section 236 portfolio. Many other properties financed under other affordable housing programs are also in need of preservation. Many of these properties continue to be "at risk" to conversion to market rate housing or are in crucial need of updating, repairs and energy upgrades. These aging properties are approaching the end of their use restrictions, in most cases within the next few years.

We all know that it is much less expensive to preserve an existing asset than to build a new one. We think HUD should be embracing the success of the Section 236 de-coupling program and utilize the same preservation tools for these other portfolios. In most instances, HUD has the statutory and regulatory authority to implement the required preservation tools for other affordable programs.

The critical tools that made the de-coupling program a success include:

- A budget based rent increase which includes new debt service.

This upfront analysis and setting of rents is critical to get lenders and equity providers comfortable with any preservation transaction. Unfortunately, the Section 8 guidelines do not allow for budget based rent increases to include new debt service to be used in calculating rents, which would be capped at post rehab market levels. Without the ability to know what rents HUD will pay it is extremely difficult to finance a preservation transaction or be competitive with conventional buyers hoping to convert the property to market rate housing to the detriment of the residents and communities most in need. Again, in his recent testimony Secretary Donovan addressed this issue and pointed it out as a critical component to secure financing in a preservation transaction.

- An increased annual distribution for all preservation owners – for profits and nonprofits.

Both the Section 236 de-coupling program and the Section 202 preservation program permit an owner to receive increased distributions –a critical incentive to owners. The Section 8 guidelines in April were revised to allow for an updating of the annual distribution in certain circumstances but not all. Today, in many preservation transactions the new owner must accept the original owner's annual distribution limitation which was established in most cases more than 30 years ago and based on their original investment, not the new investment. HUD has the regulatory authority to change this for all of its properties. Deferred developer fees which may be needed to make a transaction viable can only be paid from distributable cash. Any limitation potentially interferes with the ability to pay a deferred developer fee. IRHP proposes that a cap on distributions be eliminated entirely. Any limitation only serves as a disincentive to preservation.

- Rollover of certain HUD debt.

Oftentimes when properties are being transferred to new ownership certain HUD debt including flexible subsidy loans and Mark-to-Market soft debt cannot be paid off in full. HUD guidelines allow for flex subsidy debt to be rolled over and deferred if it is necessary to make the preservation transaction economically feasible. Notwithstanding these guidelines, HUD over the past several years has required this debt to be repaid, often times making a good preservation transaction unworkable. The draft legislation allows for the forgiveness or assignment of flexible subsidy loans for a preservation developer. We urge you to include the deferral of this debt and expand it to include mortgage restructuring debt held by HUD.

These are simple, practical and workable preservation tools which have made the Section 236 de-coupling program a huge success. I point out that the average rehab in the preservation transactions we have participated in is $25,000-$35,000 per unit. The properties are recapitalized and renovated taking into consideration today's standards – increased security, lighting, energy efficient appliances and windows, new baths and kitchens, landscaping and the creation of community and learning centers. Often, owners will also provide a package of tenant supportive services, including lifestyle training, computer training and coordination with local service providers. We did this in our 2008 purchase of the 370 unit Foxview Apartments in Carpentersville, IL and our 2007 purchase of the 400 unit Villa Nueva Apartments in San Diego, CA. Both properties were preserved with a 20-year HAP contract and significantly renovated at a cost of approximately $30,000 per unit and $60,000 per unit respectively. In both cases, social service areas were renovated or built, major interior and exterior renovations were undertaken, security was improved, and at Villa Nueva solar panels were installed to supply nearly all of the electric needs for the property. These two acquisitions will provide renovated, safe, well operated housing for nearly 800 low income families for the next 20 plus years.

Madam Chairman, the draft preservation legislation incorporates the lessons learned from the Section 236 de-coupling program and sends a clear message to HUD that preservation should be a priority. Secretary Donovan has a strong record on affordable housing preservation and we believe he will implement key policies to expand preservation. The draft bill however goes even further. It includes converting RAP and Rent Supp contracts which are nearing their 40 year expiration to project-based Section 8, expands the events for providing enhanced vouchers to residents, keeps existing subsidies in properties that otherwise would be lost, and allows for increased opportunities for an owner to project base Section 8 vouchers. Further, it puts to rest HUD's controversial policy of restricting a nonprofit's sales proceeds.

IRHP applauds your efforts. It is critical, however, that all preservation developers – for profit or nonprofit – have access to the same resources – that there is a "level" preservation playing field. Preservation developers are competing for the same resources – tax exempt bonds, low income housing tax credits, and other available federal, state and local funds. The final preservation bill must maintain this evenhandedness. In this regard any abridgement of an owner's property or contract rights will have a chilling effect on preservation. The bill incorporates a federal right of purchase which has the potential to negatively affect these rights. Secretary Donovan himself noted the legal complications of a local law providing certain groups a priority to purchase affordable housing projects in New York City where he served as housing commissioner. The state courts eventually overturned the law but unfortunately preservation efforts in New York City were interrupted for 2 years. This provision should be eliminated.

Madam Chairman, thank you for providing us the opportunity to testify here this morning on this extremely important issue. IRHP and its members are committed to affordable housing.

We are committed to preservation. We look forward to working with you and Secretary Donovan in expanding the efforts to preserve affordable housing.

CHAPTER SOURCES

Chapter 1 - This is an edited, reformatted and augmented version of a Congressional Research Service publication, R41182, dated January 3, 2011.

Chapter 2 - This is an edited, reformatted and augmented version of a Testimony given by Tammye Trevino, Administrator, Rural Housing Service, U.S. Department of Agriculture, Before the Subcommittee on Housing and Community Opportunity, on July 15, 2009.

Chapter 3 - This is an edited, reformatted and augmented version of a Statement given by Toby Halliday Vice President, National Housing Trust Presented to the Subcommittee on Housing and Community Opportunity House Committee on Financial Services, on July 15, 2009.

Chapter 4 - This is an edited, reformatted and augmented version of a Statement given by Ricky Leung, Treasurer, National Alliance of HUD Tenants, Before the Subcommittee on Housing and Community Opportunity, Hearing on "Affordable Housing Preservation and Protection of Tenants", on July 15, 2009.

Chapter 5 - This is an edited, reformatted and augmented version of a Testimony of the Institute for Responsible Housing Preservation Presented by Sarah Metherell Vice President, Steadfast Companies Financial Services Committee Subcommittee on Housing and Community Opportunity U.S. House pf Representatives Hearing on Affordable Housing Preservatio, on July 15, 2009.

INDEX

D

E

F

G

H

I

J

L

Q

R

S

T

U

V

W